"More Alive Than Ever..."
Always, Karen

To Karen and Tom

"More Alive Than Ever..."
Always, Karen

EPM Publications, Inc.
McLean, Virginia

Library of Congress Cataloging-in-Publication Data

Walker, Karen, 1949-1970 (Spirit)
    More alive than ever—always, Karen / Jeanne Walker
        p. cm.
    ISBN 0-939009-86-2
    1. Spirit writings. 2. Walker, Karen, 1949-1970. I. Walker,
Jeanne, 1924-   . II. Title. III. Title: More alive than ever.
133.9'3—dc20   94-46736
                                                               CIP

EPM Publications, Inc., 1003 Turkey Run Road
    McLean, VA 22101
Printed in the United States of America

Cover and book design by Tom Huestis

Contents

Introduction

I GLADLY ASSENTED when asked to write this Introduction not only because of the close friendship that has developed since my first meeting at Christmas, 1970, with Tom and Jeanne Walker but also because I have a spiritual teaching background of more than forty years. I feel that I can help the reader to visualize something of the setting from which Karen communicates, since hers is a situation that we all have to meet sooner or later but know little or nothing about.

I want to assure the reader that what the writer of this book claims to be the communicated thoughts of her daughter has the authentic ring of truth. When Mr. Walker called me for a first appointment, I said, "I am being told I must see you"; at that time it had already been decided in the spirit world that this book had to be written.

This book had to be written as a part of the spirit world plan to quicken intelligent interest in a life following physical death. Prevalent ideas picture the end of earth-life as an end in itself and a severance forever from those we love. That is a very poor conception indeed of Creation; and, so far as Christian thought and teaching are concerned, it shows utter failure to evaluate Christ's answer to the penitent thief, "Verily I say unto thee, *today* shalt thou be with *me* in paradise." Rebirth into a world of spirit is clearly shown as the birthright of every living soul, and it is in no way conditional upon religious beliefs or personalities.

It is from the place to which both saint and sinner went in spirit from the Cross that Karen writes. To students of metaphysics, paradise is better known as the astral, and it is important that I write something about it. It is that area of life eternal in which sooner or later we shall all find ourselves. It interpenetrates earth with all the atomic vibrations that go into making up

THE REVEREND GEORGE DAISLEY

our physical planet; it is also a duplicate of earth—but without the environmental desecration. What I am saying is that all the continents of earth, its rivers, mountains, places, and every form of nature we know is reflected in the astral. While this may seem incredible, it is only further proof that truth is stranger than fiction and is a much more logical interpretation of creation and death than is currently thought.

The basic difference between earth and the spirit world is vibrational. We cannot see into the afterlife with physical vision because its rate of vibrations is too high, but the world of spirit can discern all that goes on here; so those interested in a particular area of earth—home and loved ones, for instance—can keep themselves informed. They are aided further because we of earth exist in "duplicate," a fact of which most are ignorant despite the fact that St. Paul said to the Corinthians that we have not only our physical frame but also a spirit body that carries its own illumination, known as the aura. "There is a natural body, and there is a spiritual body" (I Corinthians 15:44).

Because our thoughts are to the world of spirit as objective as speech is to us on earth, Karen was also able to listen in to what her parents were thinking. The careful reader will observe time and again that the author found her daughter giving the answer that complemented questing thoughts. It is most essential that I make clear at once the fact that although Karen knew what her mother was thinking, her thoughts were on a closed circuit, so to speak. Thus privacy is maintained.

Karen says that all on the other side of life are young. This is true; age is restricted to the physical body, which is burned or otherwise obliterated when it ceases to house the living spirit. This withdraws in its spirit body to the world of spirit where it manifests as a mature being if it has had a long enough earth life. If it was a young life, it grows over the years to maturity, and schooling forms part of the growing process.

Karen talks about guides. It was a guide of mine who told me I had to see the Walkers. It should be understood that the afterlife is a highly organized and well-governed stage of existence. I am what is known as a test medium, with clairvoyant and clairaudient gifts of the spirit; I can both hear spirit voices and see the speakers. The Prophet Samuel was outstanding as a test medium in the Old Testament, and in more recent times, Joan of Arc was one.

Although I did not know at the time why I had to see the Walkers, the decision to write the book through Karen had already been made in furtherance of spirit world plans. In the Walker family they knew they had found a rare combination that could be helpful to humanity once the family had been separated by death; and the youngest of the "Three Musketeers" had awakened to life's realities on the other side of life. Here was a very intelligent girl who through ill health had been frustrated in almost every legitimate aim to make use of education and a loving family background. When she realized that she had an active life before her still, there was no holding her back. But first it was necessary to repair the damage her passing had left on this side of life. That was where I as a medium came into the picture.

Karen was fortunate in having highly educated and cultured parents with inquiring and flexible minds able to grasp and appreciate the advanced teachings that Karen was being helped to communicate without carrying credulity beyond the bounds of their natural good sense. Jeanne was sensitive enough to become the recording agent through automatic writing and to question mentally anything that seemed to outrun logic. That is a feature that makes this book of such value: it informs, it teaches, and it clarifies while still retaining the qualities of a story with a potential for untold good. Tom's temperament was valuable in the complementary sense, and his detachment enabled him to make his contribution when doubt or indecision on a particular aspect assailed the scribe. The "Three Musketeers" are a tower of strength because they were bound together in earth life as a family in a way few families have been and thus still form together one instrument attuned to give and receive notes of wisdom from the world that is *not* Beyond, but *here* and *now*.

The Reverend George Daisley

Acknowledgments

MY SPECIAL THANKS to several people who made this book possible: to Hilary Roberts, Research Producer of Unsolved Mysteries who believed "the story of Karen Walker was extraordinary"; to my wise and considerate editor and publisher, Evelyn Metzger, whose persistence in getting it published never wavered; to Jim Alvarado and George Daisley whose loving cooperation made it happen; and especially to Tim O'Sullivan whose advice and support I cherish. He always knew that someday Hollywood would call.

PART ONE

Karen's Life Beginnings

1

CHAPTER

THE CANCER STARTED in Karen's right thigh when she was twenty. It spread through the blood into other parts of her body. She fought the disease with all her energy for one year and died of Ewing's sarcoma at twenty-one.

She lived a normal life here; when she returned from the other side of life, she became unique.

I am Jeanne, Karen's mother. Tom was her father. Jim was her fiance.

The Walkers lived average, uninterrupted lives. Nothing out-of-the-ordinary happened, nothing terrible, either.

During Karen's first thirteen years, Tom was a Congregational minister in various churches in Southern California. He did a superb job: he increased the membership of one church from two hundred to eight hundred; he led a youth group attended weekly by more than a hundred teen-agers; he counseled the sick, troubled, bereaved; and he preached inspiring and intellectual sermons. We considered ourselves liberal. In retrospect, we were considerably bound by religious orthodoxy.

I rebelled against becoming the traditional minister's wife who attended women's meetings, taught a Sunday School class, and played the piano for services. Instead, I found my niche in church life by leading a prayer group, for I believed in prayer as a mystic search for God as well as a power for changing life's circumstances. One profound mystical experience had left me with a sense of humility and awe toward the universe. Prayer for healing seemed to work when I used it for minor illnesses.

Both Tom and I believed in life after death, certainly a Christian doctrine. We were sufficiently liberal that we had read a book or two in the psychic field. Just before Karen died I had read *The Other Side* by Bishop James Pike. We had once attended a lecture by the famous medium Arthur Ford. But these experiences were more intriguing than satisfying, and our knowledge of the psychic was certainly limited. Our conviction about the survival of bodily death was intellectual, academic—a logical and reasonable assumption and nothing more.

Then Tom became ill, and he left the ministry. With a sigh of relief, we all gained a sense of freedom as we moved from the restrictive glare of church life into other work. I became a high school English teacher. After a period of rest and recuperation, Tom taught English at the local community college.

We moved from the parsonage into our own house in Alta Loma, adjacent to the foothills and about forty miles from Los Angeles. In winter snow-covered mountains inspired us, and occasionally the snow descended to our backyard. In summer the Santa Ana winds often made us miserable until the wind shifted and an ocean breeze refreshed us.

Life became serene and purposeful. Tom and I had fulfilling jobs. I pursued hobbies—painting, weaving, writing. Karen attended high school, made new friends, and looked forward to college. She attended football games and dances. In her senior year she became the yearbook editor.

Even in our new lives, the three of us remained close. The ministry had brought us uniquely together. The more the church had impinged on our public lives, the more we had pulled together into a loving family unit. The one change in that unity came in Karen's senior year when she started dating Jim. Over the next three years he became so much a part of our family that we were four, not three.

At Christmas, 1969, our ordered, vital world began to self-destruct. As the cells multiplied randomly in Karen's body, the structured cells of our world went rampant. For a year anxiety and pain devoured our lives. Then it ended. When Karen's death was fact, no academic conviction about continued life satisfied us. Tom and I needed help; we found it, and we shared that help with her fiancé, Jim.

We discovered the Reverend George Daisley, the well-known medium who helped us get in touch with Karen. Through him, our belief in her survival on another plane became absolute.

I am well aware that the impact of our sittings with Reverend Daisley is far greater on us and on those who knew Karen than it will be on the reading public. The meaning of the best evidence of life after life is relevant only to those most concerned. However, I tell of these sittings in all honesty and sincerity. Tom and I *know* we have talked with our daughter, and we feel others will be helped by this knowledge.

Also, my own mediumship gradually developed over the years and further convinced us. This took the form of automatic writing, with Karen apparently controlling my pen. Sounds weird? Believe me, I thought so too.

It happened this way. After Karen's death, I had tried to write a book about her. I knew that the story of Karen's illness was not very different from that of thousands of others, and that our family faced the same problems and heartaches that countless other families have faced. Yet each time I looked at her schoolbooks on the shelf, each time I saw her clothes hanging in the closet, I again felt the urge to tell about her. So I tried.

For weeks I prowled through her scrapbooks, photo albums, and journals trying to decide what to include. I outlined and re-outlined. When I finally wrote, it was terrible. I stashed the manuscript and gave up.

One day as I was writing my notes for class, the pen began to scribble letters that ran together. They looked like this.

momyou'retoosentimentalandimnosaint

ifyouletmeithinkcantellmystorythroughyou

I thought I had lost it. Then as I stared at the jumble, I realized it said, "Mom, you're too sentimental, and I'm no saint. If you will let me, I think I can tell my story through you."

Karen was offering to help me tell about her?

Well, OK. I could deal with that—let her use my pen and obviously my mind as well.

Within days the writing separated itself into words. Next I began knowing what the pen was going to write before it wrote. That worried me, for I could be doing the writing instead of Karen. Eventually, to prevent coloring the messages with my own thoughts, I learned to develop a kind of double consciousness. I deliberately thought about some project such as preparing a lecture for class. Then the pen could run on of its own accord with little conscious interference from me.

That helped.

In telling about her life before she died, she directed my thinking to the particular stories she felt were important, yet I did the actual writing.

On occasion, however, as for example when I didn't know how she had perceived an event, she actually wrote in her own words. I had little knowledge of her inner feelings during her illness. Those she described herself.

For a time the writing struggle stopped; the words flowed from my pen without hesitation. The story and ideas literally wrote themselves.

Then my struggle took a different form. I often interrupted the writing because of the deep emotion that surfaced. I had to drop the pen because I could take no more. Of course this suggests my unconscious was seeking a catharsis. If indeed it is my own unconscious, I owe the reader an apology for unintentional egotism.

I don't know which is the answer. Probably both.

Karen also gave glimpses of her life in her new world. And eventually she gave teaching messages. These offered perspective on how the functioning of her world affects ours, how we can learn to use that knowledge to our advantage, how we can prepare ourselves to function effectively in her world when our time comes.

Intriguing.

But again I balked.

I said aloud, "Karen, how will I know the writing isn't just my imagination making up ideas? Maybe my unconscious mind is working overtime."

The jumbled writing answered, "Don't worry about it. You will soon discover the ideas are not ones you have thought of before, but they will make sense to you and to our readers."

I talked to my very analytical, very intelligent husband. Tom read some of the messages about ThoughtForms and said, "The pen is writing some most interesting and profound thoughts. If Karen is doing it, then we have a wonderful contact with another world." He laughed. "If it is your subconscious, then I'm proud of you. You have hidden talent and depth I never suspected."

However, as Karen concerned herself with the concepts and teachings she and her colleagues wanted to convey, I wanted proof that Karen was really communicating through me.

I had to know that the automatic writing came from an outside source, not my unconscious mind.

I could tell myself that I wasn't knowledgeable enough about metaphysical matters for the ideas to be mine; I could accept Tom's judgment that the pen was writing interesting and profound thoughts and the source didn't matter; I could get confirmation through Reverend Daisley's mediumship—but all that rationality wasn't enough. I wanted evidence.

I asked and waited. Finally, apparently trying to offer me documentation of her control of my pen, Karen wrote a message about future events that I couldn't possibly have known. She said that her friends Carole and Jerol were both expecting babies. If true, this was news to me. Further, she said that Carole's baby would be a girl and Jerol's, a boy.

I waited longer. Birth announcements finally arrived. The writing was accurate. But then my skepticism took over again. The two young women were obviously at the right time of life to have babies. The chance of boy or girl was fifty percent. I decided I had been lucky.

Karen tried again. After Karen died, Jim had completed his BA degree in biology.

"Get an MA," urged Tom. "You may want to teach at the college level or become an administrator."

He helped Jim apply at the University of Arizona at Flagstaff, where Tom's father had taught. Tom helped him get a scholarship, and we found the rest of the money for expenses.

About October, Karen's automatic writing said, "Jim plans to drop out of school. Because you've invested so much in him, he will try to finish the semester. You should know that he has found another girl."

None of that surprised me.

Karen added, "Both decisions are all right with me."

I stayed quiet about the message and waited.

Jim did make it through one lonely semester—a Southern California boy transplanted from sunshine to ten-foot snow banks at an altitude of almost 9000 feet. If he had a girl, he said nothing to us. He phoned often and returned to visit us at the end of the fall semester.

He sat in his favorite chair in our living room, clearly suffering. "You two mean so much to me, and I don't know how to tell you."

"That you don't want to continue to the Masters degree," Tom surmised.

"Well, I guess I'm burned out on school right now. But it isn't just that."

"You've found another girl." I smiled approval. I glanced at Tom and silently urged his support. He smiled and said nothing.

"How . . ."

". . . did I know?" I grinned at Jim. "A scribbling pen told me."

Jim couldn't get over his guilt so easily. "I still love Karen. I always will."

I walked over and hugged him. "What's the girl's name?"

"Kathy."

I don't think I ever got around to telling Jim how I knew.

Again I was pleased that the writing was confirmed—sort of. Karen had certainly told me some facts long in advance of their happening. But knowing human nature (and considering what a clever person I am!), I thought I could have predicted these events myself.

I still hoped for more evidence.

One day as I read over the material Karen had written, I found a strange message embedded in the middle of a paragraph on ThoughtForms. It read, "Beany's here now. We talk a lot."

Beany? I hadn't seen Karen's school friend Beany since he visited Karen when she was ill. He hadn't contacted me after she died, but that didn't surprise me, for I knew he was surely devastated. Now she seemed to be saying he had died too.

I didn't want to upset his mother by asking. About a week later I saw a friend who knew Beany's family slightly. During our conversation, she said, "By the way, had you heard that Karen's friend Beany died recently? He died of cancer, too, only much more rapidly than Karen. He lived about three months after the disease was diagnosed."

Without doubt Karen and Beany had much to talk about.

At last I could believe that the writing came from Karen.

Many times over the years I have received further confirmation of the accuracy of the messages, but the information about Beany convinced me.

About ten years ago Karen had to adjust to my new writing habits. I became a computer person, and wrote my class notes, memos, and essays in this easier mode. She didn't hesitate for an instant. She abandoned the clumsy pen and now directs my fingers on the keyboard.

I have finally reached a level of confidence in the writing so that I no longer need the state of double consciousness. This allows me to enter into dialogue with Karen. Often I stop the writing and ask questions. As we converse, she can clarify whatever concept may seem puzzling. Because I concentrate more on the messages than on the keyboard, typos abound. Karen says, "Thank goodness for spelling tools."

She even went so far as to modify her vocabulary. What she had once called thought-forms became ThoughtForms. When I noticed the change, she said, "How's that for using computer lingo, Mom?"

Regardless of the source of the messages—whether through Reverend Daisley's mediumship or my writing—I believe they are important. Karen's struggle with life and death is a universal one, and she met it gracefully. Her thoughts about life, whether in our world or hers, offer much for us to ponder.

During that entire frustrating year as Karen fought the cancer, she seldom complained. A bright, naive girl left home to go to college in September 1969; a mature young woman stepped into her exciting new life in December 1970.

Karen's story has brought hope to others. Through the Reverend George Daisley, she was able to return and assure us of her continued life. When my book, *Always, Karen,* was published in 1975, I received many hundreds of letters testifying to the hope it had inspired.

Other letters also asked for clarification and amplification of the teachings. These came over time, and they are here now in this new book. *"More Alive Than Ever . . ." Always, Karen,* uses new language, new episodes, new evidence, and expanded teachings to retell Karen's story and to interest a new generation of readers.

2

CHAPTER

WHEN KAREN WAS GROWING UP, our family of three lived in various towns and cities in Southern California: Perris, Ontario, and Alta Loma. All of these places are within forty miles or so from Los Angeles, the beach, and, definitely, Disneyland. Not bad.

Karen's father, Tom, was a Congregational minister at that time. Probably more than with any other profession, preachers' kids, PKs, are often given special treatment. (Here comes the bragging.) Church members thought Karen's naturally curly auburn hair, large hazel eyes, and round, angelic face made her adorable. They pampered her. She took advantage of that. What kid wouldn't love special treats, extra gifts for birthdays and Christmas, and constant attention?

But being a PK has its downside too. Adults expect PKs to be as good and pure as their fathers. They expected Karen to be as angelic as she looked. She rebelled. She didn't want to go to Sunday School. She squirmed when she sat beside me in church services. When parishioners invited us to their homes for dinner, she preferred to stay at home with a sitter. Although the church members often disapproved, Tom and I let her make those choices. We wanted her to be independent.

Sometimes her choices shocked me. At those times I had to watch myself that I didn't force my wishes on her without reason. For instance, when Karen was about thirteen, her paternal grandfather died. Her grandparents lived with us at that time. On the day of his funeral, she asked me if she had to attend.

I started to say, "Of course you must." Instead, I waited long enough to try to find out her reason.

I said, "I think your grandmother will be hurt if you don't. Why don't you want to go?"

"I don't think people really die," she said. "I mean, I think they keep on living somewhere, but I don't think that place is Heaven or Hell. I think they stay close." She finished in a rush. "I don't think Granddad will be at that funeral parlor or in that coffin. I think he will be right here in this house, and that's where I want to be."

It made sense. Still, I worried about her grandmother's reaction. I said, "Why don't you explain that to your grandmother and see what she says?"

Karen did discuss this with Grandmother who was gracious but obviously disappointed. She said, "You shouldn't run away from unpleasant duties."

Karen denied that as her motive. "Please understand, Grandmother. I really believe Granddad will be here."

Later she told Grandmother and me about the happening. "At ten-thirty, when the funeral was going on, I was sitting in my room, thinking about Granddad. All of a sudden I heard the coffee pot rattle in the kitchen." She smiled at Grandmother. "You know it only made that sound when Granddad poured coffee; it didn't rattle for anyone else. I was alone in the house, and I thought I was hearing things. I stayed quiet. About ten minutes later, it happened again." She looked embarrassed but triumphant.

I asked her, "What did you do?"

"I went into the kitchen and said out loud, 'Granddad, I know that's you rattling the coffee pot, but you're scaring the hell out of me, so cut it out, please.' Sorry for swear word, Grandmother, but I did say 'please.'"

"Did the noise stop?"

"Right after I said it, it clattered once more, very loud. Then it stopped. You see, he's still here."

Grandmother only shook her head.

The day following the funeral, Grandmother joined us for breakfast. Karen, probably trying to make things right with her grandmother, poured her a cup of coffee. The pot made no sound.

Grandmother took a sip and sighed. "I heard it too," she said.
"Heard what?" I asked.

"I couldn't sleep last night, so I came into the living room to
read. Ed rattled the coffee pot." She looked embarrassed. "I
wasn't sure, so I spoke aloud to him. 'If that's you, Ed, rattle that
thing again.' About thirty seconds later, it clattered. I waited and
asked once more and it happened the third time." Tears came
into her eyes. "Maybe you were right, Karen." That was all she
ever said.

Letting Karen assert herself helped her become more her own
person. This also drew the three of us closer together. When
Karen was in junior high school, Tom insisted that she read one
of his favorite classic books, *The Three Musketeers*. He made the title our family motto. He often said, "We're the Three Musketeers,
and we will always stick together."

But I'm getting ahead of my story. Let's go back to when
Karen was my little girl. Here's the monkey story Karen insisted
I tell in detail.

My red-haired kid ran in the front door. "Mom," she yelled,
"can I have a banana?"

I was always delighted when my three-and-a-half year old
Karen would eat fruit, but I was puzzled. "Of course, but you
just finished breakfast. Are you hungry already?"

"It's not for me. It's for the monkeys."

What an imagination. Always making up stories. I ruffled her
short red curls affectionately, and I pretended to play along.
"How many monkeys?"

She refused to let me doubt her game. "Two," she said, "a
mommy and a daddy. Come and see."

She took two bananas from the fruit bowl, grabbed my hand,
and pulled me through the screened-in front porch into the yard.

She hadn't made up a story.

Two monkeys, at least as large as Karen, stood in the shade of
the maple tree. She let go of my hand and started toward them. I

lunged, caught the elastic band on her shorts, and pulled her back. I didn't want to frighten her, but the animals were huge and could be dangerous. I kept my voice calm. "Why don't we get acquainted first," I said.

"I've already talked to them. They're my friends."

They probably were her friends. Karen made friends with every dog in the neighborhood, so why not monkeys? Still, I couldn't take the risk.

I reasoned with her. "They must belong to someone," I said. "Maybe their owner would not want us to feed them. In fact," I now made up my own story, "he's probably very worried about them. Let's call the police and ask."

Karen knew and liked the police chief of our small town, Perris. Chief Cox attended our church where Tom was the minister. I coaxed her into the house while I called. The woman who answered said that the chief and his deputy were out on a robbery investigation. She assured me that she would have them come as soon as they returned.

Karen went into the yard, and I followed. The monkeys had now gone into the large grassy area between our house and the church. We watched and they jumped about and chattered at one another as they moved even farther away.

"They're leaving," Karen wailed. "I want them to stay. Can't we just put a banana on the ground and see if they come back?"

Her pleading got to me. I said, "It's such a hot day, they probably would like water more than a banana."

We filled a bucket with water, set it in the yard, and returned to the safety of the porch to watch. The bold male monkey investigated, drank from the bucket, and danced a small jig of delight.

Karen's eyes danced too. "See, Mom, Paul is friendly. He likes us now."

I grinned at her. "And what did you name the other one?"

"Pearl," she answered immediately. "Let's catch them for the owner."

It seemed like a reasonable idea at the time.

I tried to imagine how to catch two monkeys. Perhaps we

could use water and bananas as bait and the screened-in porch as the cage. We could prop open the door and once Paul and Pearl went inside, we could close it.

We moved the bucket inside and put the bananas beside it. I tied a long cord to the screen door and held it open. The monkeys returned to see what we were up to. In a minute Pearl went inside and drank from the bucket. She turned and chattered to Paul. He stuck his head through the door, then backed away. Pearl started outside too. In an instant, I made the decision. If I caught her, Paul would stay nearby and the police could catch him later.

I let go of the cord, the door slammed shut, and the latch closed. Karen's caper of joy now imitated Paul's dance.

Suddenly both monkeys became agitated. Paul swung from one tree to the ground and back to another tree. Pearl bounced across the walls and ceiling of the porch. They no longer chattered. They screamed.

I wanted to open the screen door and let Pearl go, but I feared that the angry Paul might attack me if I tried. In fact, at that moment, he charged in our direction. I scooped up Karen and ran for our car in the driveway, my heart pounding. Paul shook his fist at us as we sat safely inside.

"Can't you let her out, Mom?" Karen apparently regretted her decision to catch them.

I wished I could. I imagined the female tearing up the screen and escaping. I imagined the male attacking the car and somehow breaking a window.

We watched the monkey show for another five minutes before Chief Cox finally arrived. He took in the situation and approached our car on the side away from the male. "Better stay where you are for now," he said.

I nodded. I had no intention of moving. "Can you let the monkey out?"

He shook his head. "The owner lives a couple of miles up the road. I called him, and he said they can be dangerous. He won't even come."

I wondered why a man would keep dangerous animals if he was afraid of them.

Chief Cox said, "I don't want to get near that male, but I've got a lasso pole in the car. If you would let me go into the house through the back, I think I could reach through the front door and catch her."

That sounded good to me. He ordered the deputy to drive the police car near the back door. He hoped the male monkey would remain near the front and he could take Pearl out the back.

It didn't work quite as it should have.

Cox, wearing gloves, slightly opened the front door that led from the living room to the front porch. In his hand he held a long pole with a noose on the end. The idea was to slip the noose over Pearl's head and pull it tight around her waist. He dangled it over her. She stared at it, then jumped at Cox. In an instant she scrambled across his shoulder and into the house.

Karen squealed in delight. "Mom, Pearl's in our house. Let's go."

I persuaded her that we should wait. "We don't want to get in Chief Cox's way."

Ten long minutes later, Cox emerged through the back door with Pearl tied up. He put the poor frightened thing behind the wire barrier in the back of the police car. Paul clambered up a tree and shouted monkey swear words at everyone.

With Paul up the tree and the men below to distract him, Karen and I left the car and circled the other side of the house. As we walked past the police car near the back door, Karen looked sadly at Pearl tied up inside the car. She had tears in her eyes as she said, "I love you, Pearl. I'll ask the chief to find you a home."

The police and the men from the animal shelter insisted that the monkeys' owner bring a cage. Next, they sent for a fire truck. While they waited for the equipment to arrive, Chief Cox said to Karen. "You found some pretty strange playmates, kid."

"I made friends with them," she answered. "Can you find them a good home?

The chief looked at me and shook his head. "Maybe you two should go inside," he suggested. Then he added, "I'm afraid things are pretty messed up in there."

I nodded and took Karen's hand as the fire truck rolled up. Karen held back, looking worried. She tugged on Cox's pant leg. "What are you going to do?" Perhaps she thought they might set the tree on fire to get Paul down.

The chief looked down at the concerned face under the auburn curls and smiled. "Just turn the fire hose on him."

Karen herself played in the hose on hot days. She giggled at that idea.

She giggled again when she saw the monkey paw prints that covered the walls and ceiling of the living room. Lamps lay toppled on the floor. More paw prints climbed the wall behind the refrigerator. It had been shoved into the middle of the kitchen. Filthy bath towels lay in heaps on the floor.

Outside, the men prepared to capture monkey number two.

I scrubbed my house.

Karen watched through the window when the men turned the fire hose on her friend Paul. They shot a stream of water up into the tree. Paul screamed and leaped to a nearby tree. The hose followed him. Unable to escape the force of the water, he scampered to the ground. The men were ready. Hoses attacked him from two directions, driving him tumbling and screaming into the cage. A fireman slammed the cage door shut. Paul lay curled inside, not moving.

"Is Paul hurt?" Karen asked.

About that time Paul stood up, fists clenched, and started screaming again. Clearly he wasn't hurt, only angry.

Karen had complete sympathy for Paul and fury at his captors. "Mom, how could they be so mean?" She insisted her way would have worked. "They could have used a banana."

It probably would have worked for Karen, the animal lover. She finally forgave Chief Cox when he came to tell us that the monkeys would be given to a zoo.

Karen loved it when an article appeared in the local paper. The headline read "Monkey Business at the Parsonage" and showed a picture of the male monkey in a tree.

❀ ❀ ❀

Whenever we visited the Los Angeles zoo, Karen expected also to take a pony ride at the nearby park. She always waited for her favorite pony, Brownie. She soon outgrew ponies and graduated to horses. By that time a trip to the zoo meant that she and Tom would rent horses and ride along the Los Angeles River and up through the rough hilly area of Griffith Park.

At age ten, Karen wanted a horse of her own, but we lived in a city. We would have had to board the animal permanently, and that we couldn't afford. She settled for taking riding lessons. You would think a California girl would want to ride western style, but not Karen. She preferred posting as Elizabeth Taylor had done in *National Velvet*. She became very good at it and sometimes performed in exhibitions. I suspected that what she really liked were the jodhpurs, the black fitted jacket, and the cap.

Karen loved dogs more than any other animal, and many lived in our neighborhood. The church and our house took up half the block. In the five other houses lived people with no children, so Karen had no neighborhood chums. Dogs became her playmates instead. By the time she was four, she knew all the neighbors, and they allowed her to collect their dogs and bring them to our house.

Each morning Karen held school. She called them all by name. "Clem, Marky, Tweezer, Penny, Gina. Everybody sit." They sat in a row like pupils in a class. She told them, "Now you have to learn a song." And they paid close attention as she sang.

Because her father was a minister, she knew all about weddings. From an old window curtain, she made a bridal veil for the little terrier, Gina. She put a bow tie around the neck of the beagle, Clem. She recited the wedding ceremony that she had memorized because she had heard her dad say it many times.

The dogs must have believed in the marriage because eventually Gina had a litter of puppies that looked like both Gina and

Clem. The neighbor who owned Gina gave one to Karen, and she named him Snuffy. He may not have been a good choice for a small child, for he was too young to train. If someone accidentally left the gate open, Snuffy charged into the street.

My mother, Gram, was visiting us one morning when Karen came in from play and said, "I think Snuffy's dead. The big tractor hit him, and he just doesn't move."

I had heard a tractor go by earlier. I looked out the window and saw that she was right. I wasn't sure how to help my young child adjust. Gram took over and did a great job. She held Karen on her lap and described a perfect doggy heaven. "He'll have lots of other dogs to play with and bones to chew."

"Will he find another little girl to play with?"

"I'm sure he will."

When Tom came home for lunch, he and Karen and Gram buried Snuffy under the big backyard tree where she had her tree house. Gram taught her a prayer to say when friends die.

Karen seemed satisfied that Snuffy was cared for, but she still wanted a dog of her own. Later that day I found Karen sitting on the back steps with her arm around Marky, one of many dogs owned by a family across the street. I heard her explain to Marky all about Snuffy and dog heaven and the prayer. Then she added, "Now Marky, I need a new dog, and you have to be my new dog."

I tried to tell Karen that we would get her another dog and she mustn't take one that belonged to the neighbors. But Marky was hers. Karen and Marky both knew something I didn't understand. He never again went back across the street. Finally Tom talked with the neighbors. They were happy to give Marky to Karen.

When Karen was about eight, Amber joined Karen and Marky. She was a lovably stubborn dachshund, named Amber for her reddish-gold color. The love between Karen and Amber was instant and deep. The summer Karen was ten, she went to camp in the mountains and left Amber behind. Amber spent the entire time lying on the foot of Karen's bed. She refused food. I tried to coax her to play, but she wouldn't budge. I fed her small amounts of food by hand. She ate barely enough to stay alive. When Karen returned after ten days, that very weak, excited dog almost knocked the girl off her feet and smothered her with kisses.

We knew that Amber had been born on March 22. Every year Karen celebrated that day with her dog. She always wrapped up a doggie toy or two. Although she knew sweets were bad for dogs, on Amber's birthday she broke the rules and gave her a cupcake with candles.

Stray dogs somehow found their way to Karen. Once a German shepherd wandered into our yard. Because the people at the Humane Society couldn't find any record of the dog's license in our city, they offered to take the dog for a few days while they searched other cities. Karen wouldn't hear of it. *She* would take care of Wolfgang, as she called him. Three days later we had the phone number of the owner in Los Angeles, forty miles away.

Karen insisted that the man must pick up Wolfgang after three in the afternoon when she got home from school. When he arrived and she saw the joyful reunion of man and dog, she was overjoyed. The man's story thrilled her even more. He and the dog had been hiking in the mountains beyond our city. The dog was obviously trying to find his way to Los Angeles. Karen saved him from having bruised paws from the forty mile hike.

However, when an article appeared in the local paper giving Tom credit for finding the lost dog, Karen was furious. The credit should have been hers.

3

CHAPTER

"MOM, YOU ALWAYS SAID, 'Karen is the perfect only child; she lives fully in her world.'"

The pen in my hand scribbled the words I had often spoken. The pen and I were right. Karen savored every moment of life.

When Karen was three, she and Tom lay beneath the Christmas tree staring up into the branches. She discovered her balloon-shaped face in the shiny balls. She mugged and giggled and spun stories for an hour.

On a spring day, as Karen sat on the back steps watching yellow butterflies, she began to talk to one. She held out her hand, forefinger extended. "Come here, Princess." She waited, talking softly. In a minute, Princess landed on her finger. Karen walked about the yard with her winged friend, discussing the flowers, the trees, her swing. She introduced Princess and Snuffy.

She could easily amuse herself in her own world.

Karen loved holidays, especially her own birthday. In her elementary school years, she insisted on a yearly party with her classmates. She counted on me to plan a party that would outdo those of her friends. That meant special games and a special cake. The problem was that her birthday was on January 12, the height of the rainy season in California. Each year I prayed for sunshine so the twenty or more kids could play outside. That happened once.

Fortunately we lived in the parsonage next door to the church. That made it easy to move the party to the church basement.

The church basement birthday parties gave Karen's friends the idea that the church was a great place to play. The cement floor made a perfect roller skating rink. Upstairs, the classrooms and closets were wonderful for playing hide-and-seek. No one objected to the children being there when the building wasn't being used. I did make the church sanctuary off-limits.

Only once did ten-year-old Karen and two of her friends break that rule. Late one winter afternoon they decided to play "pretend wedding." Her girlfriend, Linda, was the bride and her boyfriend, Beany, the groom. Karen, who had borrowed her father's book of ceremonies to read from, was the minister.

Karen began the ceremony. The sun rapidly faded from the huge stained glass window. The holy, mysterious, eerie room darkened dramatically. At that moment, a jangled sound came from the pipe organ. The kids froze.

"What was that?" asked Beany.

"I think it was the organ," said a scared Karen.

"Can it play itself?" asked Linda.

"Let's get out of here." Beany headed for the door.

The girls followed him. Just as they ran into the hallway, they heard the sound again. A minute later they burst into the parsonage kitchen where I was starting dinner.

"There's a ghost," shouted Beany.

They all talked at once.

Because of their obvious fright, I didn't scold them for breaking the rule about playing in the sanctuary. I suggested that we go there and try to figure out what had happened. In the big, dimly lit, silent room, the kids whispered and nervously grabbed one another. We waited about five minutes and nothing happened. I shrugged and suggested they must be imagining things.

As we started to leave, I heard it too. From the column of pipes above the organ came a noise that was part music and part moan.

I refused to accept the ghost explanation. I had no idea what it could be, but I couldn't let the kids become frightened of the church building. I phoned the organist.

"I've heard it a few times," he said, "I think the wind comes down through the pipes some way."

Karen, age 2

Karen (age 2-½) and Tom

Karen with Snuffy, the dog killed by a tractor

Karen (age 3-1/2), Betsy (doll), and Happy, one of her many dogs, 1951

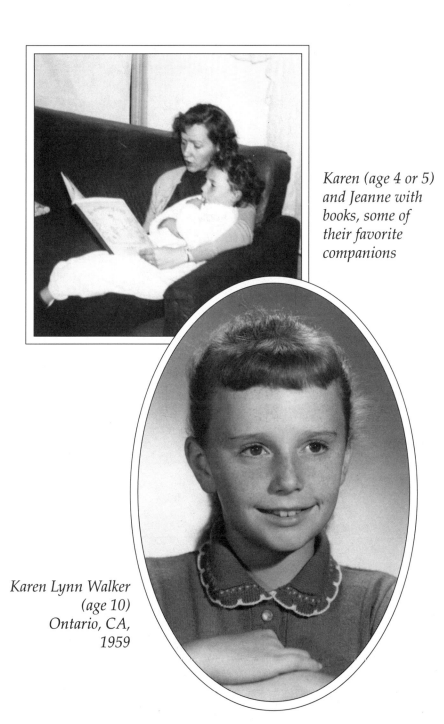

*Karen (age 4 or 5)
and Jeanne with
books, some of
their favorite
companions*

*Karen Lynn Walker
(age 10)
Ontario, CA,
1959*

Karen in ballet costume and cousin Janet at Christmas, 1956

Karen with gingerbread house (about age 10), 1960

I investigated and found a window open where wind might have blown down the pipes, but I never convinced Beany there wasn't a ghost in the church sanctuary. I'm not even sure I convinced myself. At least the kids never played in that part of the church again.

When Karen was fourteen, Tom became ill and left the ministry. For a year he was too sick to work, so I supported the family by teaching English at Alta Loma High School. Karen was just beginning high school. The three of us, all starting a new way of life, faced a choice. We could move to Alta Loma and she would attend the school where I taught, or we could move to Upland where she would not have to be identified as an English teacher's daughter.

I would have thought that after years of being a PK, she would have preferred to be unknown, but she chose Alta Loma. The only time this caused her a problem was in the eleventh grade when I taught the only section of college prep English. She had to choose between taking regular English with another teacher or advanced English with me. She chose me.

The first day of class I made a speech to the students. "You all know that Karen is my daughter. I also want you to know that she will get no special treatment in this class."

One of the boys spoke up. "Knowing your reputation, Mrs. Walker, Karen will have to work harder than any of us to earn her grade." Everyone laughed. The year worked out fine for both of us.

When Tom's health improved, he began teaching English at Chaffey College in Alta Loma. Several years later, I transferred to the college as well, and I still teach there.

And Karen? I wouldn't be bragging too much if I said she was very bright and did well in school. I have her report cards to prove it. She competed for grades and wanted to be the best. She also enjoyed taking courses that stimulated her interest.

In high school that created a problem. By the eleventh grade, her grades were high enough that she could have graduated at the top of the class and been Valedictorian. However, she wanted to take some courses where she would learn new skills (art and drama) but where she might not earn top grades. She debated the problem and decided that she preferred a variety of subjects rather than the highest grades. She graduated fifth in her class and never seemed to regret the choice.

In the tenth grade she joined the drama club. At last she could dress up and act in real plays. She was too shy to get the lead in a school play, but Tom and I attended and applauded her in her secondary roles. She had once declared that she might become an actress when she grew up. The lack of spectacular success in school plays probably changed her mind about that.

However, her success at writing encouraged her to use that skill. English was her easiest and best subject. She entered two essay contests and won first prizes. In her senior year, she joined the yearbook staff and became co-editor. That yearbook was the first at ALHS to depart from tradition and include unique picture arrangements. Especially, it was the first to include written commentary beyond the category of the "Most likely to succeed . . ." Guess who wrote those.

Her looks so absorbed her attention that I always knew where to find her—in the bathroom. She practiced putting on makeup. She could use an eyeliner as perfectly as any actress. She styled her auburn hair like Jackie Kennedy's. She studied the pages of *Charm* and *Mademoiselle* and researched the stores where she could buy the perfect boots or sweater. That usually meant a mother-daughter shopping trip to Los Angeles, and we both loved that. Somehow she managed to appear understated— "casual but elegant."

She tried other ways of making herself unique as well, like spelling her name Karyn. She finally decided that was too flashy and returned to the original spelling.

She dated. The boys included Bill, Sam, and Irwin. Bill talked of nothing but sports. Sam constantly cracked jokes. Irwin made too many fast moves. Karen looked around for someone she thought she could train to her liking. She chose Jim.

4

CHAPTER

JIM WASN'T EASY TO PERSUADE to be a boyfriend. A year younger than Karen, and shy, he had never dated. She tried to be subtle. She persuaded her high school counselor to assign her to study hall at the same hour as Jim. She rode to and from school with me and manipulated me so I parked in the lot he walked through on his way home. She would pose by the car, bored and beautiful.

Jim talked to her, but he never asked her out.

One night she dreamed about him. In the dream he stood in a crowded classroom. Suddenly he fainted and fell. He cut his face, bled a lot, and had to be rushed to the doctor for stitches. Since the female foursome shared everything, Karen told them the dream. About a week later several history classes combined to see a film. The room was crowded and stifling. Karen sat near the back where Jim was standing. As the film ended, she glanced back to spot him, hoping she could walk with him back to class. She looked, and he fainted from the heat. He didn't crumple but fell flat on his face. He cut a gash in his chin, blood poured out, and he was rushed to the doctor for stitches. Karen's girlfriends were speechless—temporarily.

Of course word got back to Jim about the dream that came true. He asked for a date. A date with Jim was an invitation to join him at the ranch where his father was a foreman. There they would hike and talk. Then they would come back to our house and raid the fridge.

Such dates caused me no worry as a mother. Neither Tom nor I objected to the fact that Jim was part Hispanic. We worried about brains. As Karen often reminded us, English teachers are snobs about intelligence and grades. We thought of Jim as a potential high school dropout. I talked to his counselor and learned that his grade point average was 2.0. That hardly put him on a level with the girl graduating near the top of the class. We waited for Karen to get bored with him.

She didn't. She admitted to me that she didn't know why she was attracted. She only said, "I admire his sensitivity. He cares about people and animals. He has more depth than the other boys I've dated."

Jim's family fascinated her. He had two brothers and three sisters. All were married except Jim and his twin sister, another redhead. Jim, his father, and one brother were dark and tall. Jim's mother and the rest were short and red-haired.

As an only child, Karen could hardly believe Sundays at their house. They all gathered, talked, ate, and enjoyed each other. They celebrated every holiday. The occasions included a large numbers of aunts, uncles, cousins and other assorted relatives. The hubbub was tremendous. These dates were as entertaining for Karen as movies and dinners out would have been.

Karen and Jim attended the Senior prom together and went with their class to Disneyland after the graduation ceremony. Tom and I were patient. She would be leaving for college in the fall. She would find many interesting young men there.

At this point Karen made the last two major decisions of her school years.

First, she changed her mind about which college to attend. She had been accepted at several of the branches of the University of California and had chosen Santa Barbara. Because Tom and I both worked, we could not expect that Karen would receive a scholarship or a grant, so we had saved our money to give her this opportunity. But Karen kept worrying about Jim. She knew that without her he would get a job and skip college.

She came to us. "Jim should have the chance at a college education too," she said. "I know he won't do it without me, so I want to go to Chaffey. I'll transfer later." She continued with arguments about how she could get a good education at a community college like Chaffey.

We needed no persuasion about that. We knew the classes were smaller than those at the university, and she would get individual attention from excellent professors instead of from teaching assistants. We were also delighted to have her stay home another year or two. We thought she would still be attracted to other young men. To Karen's surprise, we readily agreed.

Second, Karen's nose had been broken in a soccer game during a high school PE class. It had caused breathing problems. Also, for years she had moaned about the ugly nose she had inherited from her father and grandfather. "It's not so bad on a man," she told Tom, trying not to hurt his feelings, "but it makes me look like a turtle. I really want plastic surgery."

Again we agreed. Not only would it help her breathing, but it might also help her self esteem.

She had the rhinoplasty as soon as graduation was over. All went well except that her nose unexpectedly bled so much that she needed a transfusion of two pints of blood. That transfusion might have led to the cancer.

Tom and I decided that with the money we had saved on tuition, we could afford to buy her a new small car instead of a secondhand one. We surprised her. The Three Musketeers went shopping at the Toyota agency. Karen was in ecstasy as she drove her new red Toyota to Jim's house to show off.

❀ ❀ ❀

A pattern developed. For two years Karen and Jim attended school together. They spent evenings at our house studying. The huge old desk that had belonged to her grandfather occupied the spare room, and she and Jim spent their evenings at that desk.

Because Jim's college career started at an absolute academic bottom, Karen chose herself as his tutor. She had to teach him everything, even how to take notes and read a textbook. I would listen to them from my study across the hall. She cajoled, persuaded, threatened, cried, and even kicked him on the shin to keep him trying, for there were countless times he was ready to quit. Gradually she began to win. Clearly Jim was highly intelligent; he had just never been trained to study.

Tom joined Karen's efforts with Jim before I did. He helped get Jim a scholarship for tuition and books at Chaffey. He encouraged him with pep talks. Although Jim still lived at home, he ate most dinners with us. Of course I provided snacks to encourage the hard work of learning.

Later, in the automatic writing, Karen wrote, "Finally the four of us put it across. At the end of two years, Jim left Chaffey College with a B average, and as I write this, Jim has won his Bachelor of Science degree. He was on the dean's list every semester and is now working toward his teaching credential. After my initial training, he did it all on his own, for he became a real scholar. My pride in him is boundless."

She continued writing, "But more important for me at that time, Jim's sensitivity expanded. From a sometimes introverted, immature kid, he changed into an outgoing, mature young man. I credit both of our dads for this. They provided advice and models."

She reminded me that in one instance, her dad had the opportunity to prove himself. It involved a situation that developed toward the last of their two years at Chaffey. After two years of dating only Jim, Karen apparently began to feel trapped.

She wrote, "I hadn't experienced enough contact with other boys to be sure I really loved Jim. Since we were talking about marriage, I began to panic. And because of my 'superior' knowledge and ability, I had become not just his girl friend but his mother as well. In fact, Mom, you kidded me about having an earth-mother complex and taking care of Jim. You were suggesting that Jim and I might eventually have a poor relationship, and it would be partly my fault.

"But I was sure that without my constant advice he just couldn't take care of himself. Then, suddenly, it backfired. I realized I made every decision for the two of us. I really wanted to be taken care of myself but because of my own failure, it wasn't happening."

She secretly started dating a boy in her biology class. They had nothing in common, but he was a decisive, masterly young man, and she loved it. Of course Jim found out eventually, and I'm sure she wanted him to. They spent one miserable evening in the red Toyota, arguing. They returned home about ten and asked Tom and me to arbitrate until two o'clock in the morning.

I had known that Karen was being sneaky long before Jim did. I had alerted Tom. The day following the blowup, Tom had a long talk with Jim. To this day neither Karen nor I know what he said, but Jim changed. When the fuss blew over, Karen said to Tom, "You're the best dad in the whole world."

She dated other boys for a while, and Jim came around only when invited. It didn't take long. By summer she dropped the other boys and went back to Jim.

5
CHAPTER

"I was scared, though I'm sure I didn't show it."

This was Karen's first coherent writing after she began to control my pen.

She continued, "The summer of 1969 was a bad one for me. Whether my problem was emotional or physical, I wasn't sure, but deep inside I knew I was very sick."

Karen did have a bad summer.

In the June after Karen and Jim finished their two years at Chaffey College, she decided to get a job to pay for her clothes and school supplies when she went to Chapman University.

Tom and I protested. "We'll pay for everything," we insisted. "Enjoy your vacation."

"I have to prove to myself that I've grown up. I'm twenty and still living at home. That's embarrassing."

She got a job at Farrell's Ice Cream Parlour where they hired the girls for looks and personality. On the first count she qualified. Call it a mother's lack of objectivity if you like, but Karen was a pretty girl. Her best features were auburn hair, large hazel eyes, and a very special nose. With the plastic surgery, she no longer "resembled a turtle."

As for personality, Karen felt some lacks. Farrell's expected its waitresses to make loud, enthusiastic announcements about birthdays and the like. Easily embarrassed at making a spectacle of herself, she had difficulty with that. Yet because she couldn't stand being imperfect, she overcompensated and performed well.

She had trouble with her right leg that summer. During the previous spring she had twisted it. While at first the pain had been intermittent, the waitress job aggravated it until the ache became constant. We sent her to the family doctor. His examination and X rays revealed no physical source for the pain; cortisone treatments for supposed bursitis didn't work. She limped. She lost appetite and gradually lost weight. When I questioned her, she admitted the pain seemed to be getting worse.

Apparently something else was going on inside Karen as well. In the automatic writing later she explained, "Emotionally I was confused. It is hard to explain the feelings I had at that time; they sound so abnormal. I thought about death. This occupied my thoughts so much that I believed I needed a psychiatrist. Even when I was having fun, the sudden thought of death came—not about my own death but most often about the deaths of those I loved.

"I'd had a few psychology courses; I knew what a psychiatrist would tell me. I was planning to go away to college in September, and the impending break from home was causing deep anxieties that took the form of an obsession with death. I did feel as if I were losing my home. I knew I would never live there again. I would finish school, get married, get a job.

"While I wasn't really convinced that this could cause such deep anxieties, at least this 'superior' psychological knowledge made me feel a little better. It helped explain my obsessions; at the same time it depressed me. I didn't want to tell my folks. While I could talk to them and knew they would understand, this was a part of the problem. I needed to be independent. The more concerned I became, the more I was aware that I had had these thoughts most of my life. Recently they had become more pronounced.

"I told myself, 'Quit worrying. Once you get away at school you'll be all right.' "

So Karen's summer, more traumatic than either Tom or I knew, caused her concern.

In mid-September, Tom and I returned to teaching, and Jim and Karen loaded their cars to start their new life away from home.

Karen wrote about that. "My depression didn't improve when I went away to college. I found school work easy—really too easy. Most of it bored me. Except for one psychology course I found little challenge, but I was glad for Jim's sake. He had to succeed at the four-year school.

"My leg seemed to hurt more than it had at home. I said little to Jim or to my roommates, but sometimes the pain was almost unbearable. One afternoon in late October, the pain reached a peak, and I went to the school infirmary to ask for something stronger than aspirin. They referred me to an osteopath. I came away with the same diagnosis as that of my own doctor: nothing wrong.

"The less help I received from doctors, the more depressed I became."

One day soon after Thanksgiving Karen rushed home. She had never before told us about her depression. Surprised but eager to help, Tom and I spent many hours listening. We suggested that she drop out of school and see a psychiatrist. She debated and chose to stay in school until Christmas vacation.

She said, "I have to think about Jim. I know if I don't stay, he won't either, and he might never finish college."

Tom and I protested that he would surely stay three more weeks without her. When she left to return to school, Tom reminded her of our family motto. "Don't worry, Sweetheart. We're The Three Musketeers, and we'll always stick together."

As anxious parents, we phoned several times a week. We both admitted our relief when Karen arrived home the Friday before Christmas. We would have two weeks to help her decide what to do.

"Hi, Mom, I'm here." Karen gave her usual call as she arrived home for the holidays.

We hugged, and I made motherly noises. "You've lost more weight. We need to feed you."

The rush of Christmas consumed our attention for several

days. Jim and Karen trimmed the tree that she called a "ceiling-grabber."

Later, in the writing, she recalled a particularly bad day. "Jim was busy and Mom and Dad were away with friends. I slumped back into my depression, and that scared me. I tried to think through my problems. While my leg hurt almost constantly, I couldn't see how that would depress me so, yet all the old images of death were with me that day. In the late afternoon Jim picked me up, we went out for burgers, and I still felt depressed. When you and Dad came home at about ten, I could hardly keep from crying with relief."

The next day all was well again. Gram arrived for Christmas, Karen loved having her there. Things become lively.

We traditionally opened presents on Christmas Eve: Karen, Jim, Gram, Tom and I. Karen and I usually sat on the floor like kids to open ours; this time, Karen sat in a chair, separate from the rest of us. I suspected her leg hurt more than usual, but she wouldn't admit it.

Just before I went to bed I knocked at her door. She sat on her bed crying. She blamed the tears on her leg, but I didn't entirely believe her. I gave her some pain pills, tucked her in with hot-water bottles, and opened the way for her to talk. She pushed me aside. I suspected that she cried herself to sleep.

Karen's memory of that evening came in the writing. "I had never felt so depressed. As long as I looked at the tree and its circle of light and people, I felt happy. But the minute I looked away at the edges of the circle, I became frightened. Never in all my life would I have believed I would be glad to have Christmas over."

On Christmas Day Karen didn't get out of bed because of the pain in her leg. We phoned our doctor who was not available. We saw Dr. Lewis, one of his partners. Because Lewis couldn't find our doctor's earlier records, he sent us to the hospital for X rays and lab tests. A stronger pain prescription helped Karen through Christmas Day. Nobody ate much turkey.

The next day, Dr. Lewis said more X rays were indicated. He

took Tom off to "make arrangements." I suspected the worst. He was telling Tom that Karen was seriously ill. I kept up a too-cheerful conversation with Karen to distract her while we waited.

She seemed too miserable to notice. She could barely stand, and I had to help her undress. Once she almost fainted. Finally we got her home and into bed with Gram sitting beside her.

Tom and I went to our bedroom to talk.

"It's bad," I said.

Tom nodded. "He says it's cancer. Ewing's sarcoma. He seems very sure."

I felt numb, beyond tears. "We need a second opinion."

He agreed. "I'll call Don."

Tom's brother, Don, was at that time an administrator at UC of Irvine. Through the medical school, he had many contacts.

"By all means, get another opinion," he insisted. He called the Chief of Staff of Hoag Hospital in Newport Beach.

Meanwhile I told Gram and Jim. I made the diagnosis sound tentative. Jim took Gram to the airport to fly back to Palo Alto. We promised to call them both as soon as we knew anything.

We checked Karen in to Hoag, and events moved rapidly: more X rays, more tests, a biopsy that confirmed Ewings. Because the tumor seemed isolated in the thigh, the oncologist and cancer board recommended radiation therapy, cobalt, as the preferred treatment. The X rays showed so much destruction of the bone that Karen had to walk on crutches until radiation ended and the bone had time to mend.

Through my pen, Karen was to write later: "From the day after Christmas until I left the hospital, I remember little. I went into a black world; everything and everyone became dark and far away; I could not focus on what was happening around me. The pain absorbed my attention, and I remained in my black world; I no longer thought about death. I just disappeared into blackness."

She added, "I knew about the biopsy and the diagnosis, but I kept thinking this would all end and we would go home 'in a few days' as Dad had said. I do remember pleasures. Jim was there, my greatest comfort. Other friends came to visit, and I received many flowers. My favorite flower was from Dad. The first time I was ever in a hospital, for the nose job, he had brought me a single red rose. Now he continued this and kept me supplied constantly with fresh single red roses during each succeeding hospital stay. It became his trademark."

Tom and I located a lovely house on the boat docks at Newport, within view of the hospital. During the off season, we could rent it reasonably.

In January, when school started, I took a leave of absence from my teaching. We were twenty minutes from Jim at Chapman. He came every evening to study. Tom had to drive an hour each way to Alta Loma. He came weekends and phoned daily.

Karen wrote her memory of this time. "I lived in my own world, separate from the real world. Darkness shrouded everything and everyone. I am sure you and Dad and Jim suspected little of this, for on the surface I seemed normal, and any peculiarities in my behavior could easily be explained by the illness."

She continued, "As I write this a year and a half later, I understand what happened to me in those weeks. I passed through the shadow of death. Carl Jung understood this experience. It happens to many people who are close to death. He described the depression I had experienced for many months, followed by the experience of the black world. These are preparations for the passage from one world into another and give the individual the necessary experience before it happens.

"In describing the case of a child who acted out her death in dreams a year before she actually died, Jung says,

It was as if the future events were casting their shadow back by arousing in the child certain thought forms that, normally dor-

mant, describe or accompany the approach of a fatal issue.... Experience shows that the unknown approach of death casts an adumbration *(an anticipatory shadow) over the life and dreams of the victim. (Jung, p. 75)*

Jung, a brilliant man, caught a glimpse of a universal truth that is the way of spirit. The individual passes from one world into another; she travels through a dark tunnel into light."

Tom and I determined to do our part in beating the cancer. By that time Karen weighed only 95 pounds, down from a normal weight of 115 pounds. He studied books about diet, bought health foods, and urged Karen to eat.

I believed that spiritual food was equally urgent. I had practiced prayer techniques which had in the past, in minor instances, been successful. Now the challenge was greater. By placing my hands on Karen, I could help relieve pain and the nausea from radiation therapy.

The Three Musketeers stuck together.

Karen started radiation therapy on her twenty-first birthday, January 12, 1970. After the biopsy, she was weak, still in pain, and still on crutches.

At first it worried me that she seemed not to take the therapy seriously. She knew she had a malignant bone tumor but believed it could be controlled and apparently regarded the treatment as routine. I decided to leave that impression alone, for I saw no reason to foster fear. She did talk about being sure the tumor didn't spread into the hip joint. She didn't want to remain on crutches for the rest of her life.

On her birthday, I watched Karen perform her first legal adult act on her own behalf by signing the medical release for therapy. As she crutched into the radiation room, I wiped tears from my eyes. My daughter, grown up, did not need me, yet at that moment she must depend on me for everything.

I walked behind her into the radiation chamber. It felt strangely like a tomb: large and empty but for the machine. The silence was deathlike. Mary, the technician, chatted amiably as she helped Karen onto the table. As the sessions were to be five days a week for six weeks, we all became well-acquainted.

But Karen became even better acquainted with the huge machine. She learned to talk to it. She described it as a giant animal. If let out of bounds, it could kill, but if kept under control, it could be her friend. So she sent it soothing messages to behave itself and get rid of the tumor.

And it seemed to. Two days after treatments started, the leg pain stopped. The doctors, pleased at her response to radiation, became cautiously cheerful about the outcome.

Karen had looked forward to a twenty-first birthday with a special dinner out with friends and family. Instead, the party took place at the beach house with only the four of us. I cooked Karen's favorite chicken and rice, but she didn't eat much. The lopsided cake crumbled because the oven undercooked on one side and burned on the other. We skipped the toasts, afraid that cancer, cobalt, and crutches wouldn't mix with champagne.

During the next weeks Karen made slow progress. Her leg stopped hurting. She gained weight in spite of the nausea caused by cobalt. In the off season we saw few people at the beach house, so we read, played cards, and took treatments. A large window overlooked the boat docks at Newport. As Karen felt better, we took daily walks. She crutched along the boardwalk with me ready to steady her, just in case.

Karen lived for the evenings when Jim arrived to study. I believe she wouldn't have recovered without him. And she loved the busy, noisy weekends when Jim and Tom came for two whole days and when other friends and relatives visited. Gram and Karen's cousin Janet came from Palo Alto. Carole, one of the four high school girlfriends, arrived and reminisced about former boyfriends and slumber parties. Beany came and told Karen he still had the last gingerbread house, hard as a rock and with a few candies missing. Her cousin Craig bragged about being lifeguard and as usual they argued about what Karen perceived as his immaturity.

In spite of such activity, by the end of the fifth week of therapy Karen and I were thoroughly homesick. We had left home on December 27 "for a few days" and never returned. At last she felt well enough to make the hour drive. On a Friday after therapy, we packed her little red Toyota and went home for the weekend.

Her leg wouldn't bend properly, so she sat sideways on the back seat. She should have been off crutches by that time, but radiation had prevented the bone from growing. Doctors allowed her to put about thirty pounds of pressure on the leg as she walked with crutches, a mistake in judgment that soon cost her more hours of pain and fear.

How fantastic to be home. Karen spent hours in her room and looked forward to being home for good in one more week. She and Jim talked for hours, planning their future. The spring semester had started at Chapman without Karen. It didn't matter; she knew she would be back the following fall.

She and Jim talked about getting married, perhaps as early as December. He would have his BA degree almost completed and could get a job and finish in his spare time. She could return to school, knowing that Tom and I would pay the tuition.

Tom started to protest about a marriage before they finished school, but he said nothing. I suspected he had the same thought I did: that we had married before we finished school, and it had worked out fine.

I hadn't seen Karen so happy in months.

It happened on February 22, Presidents' Day. Holidays had become a jinx: Christmas sick, the New Year in surgery, her birthday starting radiation, and now . . .

On the last morning of her glorious weekend at home, Karen's plans broke with the snap of a bone. She awakened from a sound sleep to a cracking sound and pain stabbing her leg.

The instant I heard her frantic call, I ran. "What?"

"My leg's broken."

"Can't be."

But it was. I could see the bow in her right thigh at the site of the tumor.

"Don't move," I said.

"I'm not crazy." Sarcasm covered her terror.

The doctor told Tom, "Don't move her yourself. Call an ambulance and have them lift her without moving the leg."

I held her hand on the trip back to the hospital, heading away once more from her secure world at home. She didn't speak or look at me. I followed her gaze through the ambulance window and saw the tops of trees and phone poles spinning above her. She must have been wondering if she would ever know her normal world again.

6

CHAPTER

THE CANCER HAD EATEN completely through the bone in Karen's leg.

A neurosurgeon—he called himself a carpenter, and he was a good one—opened the leg again, this time with a thirteen-inch gash. He inserted a metal pin, attached a rod to the ends of the broken bone, and screwed everything into place. The pathological break would probably take six to eight *months* to heal.

Crutching became Karen's nightmare. The doctor gave dire warnings: absolutely no pressure on the leg. A second break would be irreparable. Permanent crippling or amputation was a distinct possibility.

One positive finding scarcely mattered to her, but it did to Tom and me. A second biopsy revealed that the bone was clean, the tumor gone.

Yet new symptoms surfaced—chest pains, diagnosed as pleurisy; inability to digest food; headaches, sinus, and ear problems. When none of these responded to medical treatment, doctors wrote them off as psychological trauma caused by the shock of the broken leg. I didn't believe that for a minute. Something else had gone wrong.

Daily I phoned one doctor or another, pleading for help. "Do more tests; something is definitely wrong." No one did anything.

Finally I insisted, "We must get a second opinion."

I could almost hear the doctor's shrug over the phone. "If you insist."

We made an appointment with a Dr. Irwin at the USC medical center.

And we moved home. At least we would have the comfort of

familiar surroundings while we waited for the diagnosis of the new symptoms.

With more X rays and tests, that the doctors at the beach hadn't bothered to do, Irwin diagnosed the problem and the solution.

Karen liked Dr. Irwin. He treated her like both a patient and a daughter and took her symptoms seriously. "You have pains in your chest because the cancer has spread," he told her. "You have tumors in your lungs and spleen. Radiation won't work for this. We must get you on chemotherapy, inject chemicals that can kill the cancer throughout your body."

He described what would happen because of chemotherapy: nausea and hair loss. She wasn't eager.

"Karen, you're an adult now, so I'm going to tell you the truth. You have about a thirty percent chance to get well. At the very most, you probably have two years to live. You have no choice but to stick with me on this treatment."

For the first time she really believed she might not make it. Yet that didn't make her depressed. It made her mad—damned mad. She determined to beat this cancer.

Tom and I had reacted the same way when Dr. Irwin had told us. For the first time the news was not the least hopeful, yet as a family we responded with anger and determination. And on that day we felt our deepest love for one another. We were truly The Three Musketeers. Love and prayer seemed our best hopes now.

Karen's concern was for Jim. She would be all right. She determined that. But she wanted him to know the worst. And she wanted him to be told the way Irwin had told her, with absolute honesty and caring. She intended to do this herself until Tom explained that it wouldn't work.

"You can't tell a loved one something like this. We wanted to tell you, but Dr. Irwin did it much better. For the same reason, you shouldn't be the one to tell Jim. I'll do it right, I promise."

She knew he would. After all hadn't he talked to Jim when they broke up?

She did say one thing to Tom. "Jim has to understand that he is free to forget me; he can't be expected to remain knowing my chances."

Yet she never once doubted his decision, for she knew he would not leave her.

Tom did his usual superb job, and Jim returned from their talk to hold her close, then and in the months ahead.

The next months, in spite of the pain and frustration, were some of the happiest of Karen's life. She told me later that the darkness left. Her goal? To get well, to get married, and to live happily ever after.

We all agreed on a December wedding. This did not seem crazy to us. We decided it because we believed. We knew that by the following Christmas she could walk on her own legs, the tumors would be gone.

We acted on our faith. Jim bought Karen an engagement ring. We shopped for her wedding dress.

We put up with the tedious weekly trips to Los Angeles for chemotherapy. Every injection of the chemicals left her nauseated for two days. The crutches made any activity a chore and a dread.

"And I'm losing my hair," she mourned.

I bought her several wigs, but the colors were no substitute for her own auburn locks.

On her fourth trip to Dr. Irwin, he surprised her. In a monotone, he said, "The X rays were negative last week."

It took a minute before she understood. She couldn't move. No tumors? Happy tears rolled down her cheeks. I choked her name and hugged her.

While he gave the injection that day, Dr. Irwin, obviously

pleased, made the usual doctor comments. "We must be cautious. The treatments must continue. When you have a winning ticket, you hang on to it."

Suddenly crutches and baldness seemed unimportant. She had a chance at life again.

She and Jim set their wedding date for December 19.

We had a good summer. At last Karen could take Dr. Irwin's chemicals orally instead of shots. The X rays continued to show negative. Jim came home for two months. We shopped, Karen still on crutches, and picked out china and silver. Her three girl-friends planned a bridal shower. After our long struggle with tumors and treatments, we knew the joy of returning life.

During a shopping expedition one day, Karen discovered some Siamese twins—two cloth dolls sewn permanently together and wearing batik dresses. She laughed. "There we are, Mom. Stuck together whether we like it or not." We bought them, hoping some day we could laugh at the way things had once been.

Karen had always been a bit superstitious. When she took a philosophy class at Chaffey, an instructor introduced the class to a book called the *I Ching*, an ancient book of Chinese wisdom. The professor explained that many people used the *I Ching* to tell fortunes. Karen bought a copy and three ancient Chinese coins and tried it. It seemed to work, and from then on when she had a problem, she used the coins and the book to try to predict her future. During this year of illness, she used them often, especially during the next weeks when one doctor told her the cancer was back.

The summer brought two problems we had to live with. First, the bone in the leg didn't grow back. We still had several months before the wedding. If necessary, she could crutch down the aisle. Second, she had an ear infection. Even heavy doses of antibiotics didn't cure it. Finally, in early October, Dr. Irwin sent her to see a neurologist who did tests that seemed to her too simple to be accurate. Then he said, "You have a tumor at the base of the skull."

How could this be? Dr. Irwin's X rays, always reliable, had shown nothing. When we asked him, he said he didn't know. "X rays are sometimes slow to show tumors. The neurologist's tests show certain failures in muscular reactions and some brain damage. We have to consider the possibility that the cancer has spread."

In October he put her back in the hospital for another week of tests. On her last morning there, Dr. Irwin said, "I see no specific tumors. However, the entire spinal area shows tumorous blockage."

She didn't want to hear what he said. She consulted the *I Ching* to ask if he was right. The book never says anything so obvious as "Don't listen to your doctor." However, it did talk about meeting misfortune with fortitude and courage. She took that to mean that she was probably sicker than she wanted to believe.

By the middle of October, a tumor appeared at the base of the skull. She went daily to a hospital near home for more radiation. It didn't seem to help. By Halloween she felt miserable. By Thanksgiving she couldn't sit at the table to eat. She no longer had specific aches, but her entire body, especially her back, was in constant pain. Tumors had returned to her lungs and spleen, and now the brain. Dr. Irwin, Tom and I agreed not to tell Karen or Jim. We had told them from the first that her chances were small; there was no need to say it again.

Early in December she returned to the Orthopedic Hospital in Los Angeles for treatment. She was very sick. I stayed with her constantly and slept on a cot in her room. She went into a coma and came out of it only once.

"Mom!"

Karen's voice—the sound I had waited for more than a week

to hear—roused me. After an intolerable nine days of silence, my daughter had at last awakened from her coma.

Instantly I rose from my cot next to her hospital bed and took her hand in mine. I turned on the night light above her bed. Her eyes focused on me.

"Karen. You're back." Although I knew better than to hope too much, momentarily I felt relief and joy.

Only that morning Dr. Irwin had told Tom and me that all hope for her was gone. He had also warned us that many days of a vegetable existence might remain. Her father and I had discussed our options—rationally of course—and determined that when the time came, all unnecessary life support should be removed.

Dared I hope? Could Dr. Irwin have been wrong?

Karen nodded. "Only long enough for a chat, Mom."

My hope subsided. "Tell me."

"I've lost my power," she said.

"What power?"

"The power to think. The cancer is in my brain. I don't want to live without my mind. I couldn't stand that. You know how much I value thinking."

I squeezed her hand.

"I must go on. If I stay here, I will no longer be a person."

I stroked the wisps of her once-plentiful auburn hair that the chemotherapy had destroyed. "How can you be so sure?"

Her voice sunk to a whisper. "I've been told. I must go on. Will you let me?"

I wanted to shout at her to keep fighting.

"I'm not afraid," she said. "I know I will have a wonderful new life. But I had to be sure you were willing to let me go."

She made an effort, and her voice grew stronger. "Think about it this way. If I lived, I would eventually leave home, and you would miss me but would know I was having a good life."

It didn't seem quite that simple to me. Dying wasn't just leaving home. I would never again be able to talk to her.

56

But this was Karen asking, the Karen that Tom and I had raised to think for herself and make her own decisions. I had no choice.

I wiped the tears from my eyes. "You don't need my permission, but of course, I would not hold you back."

She gave a sigh of relief. Her eyes closed, and I thought for a minute that she had returned to her coma. She opened them again. "Tell Dad. Tell Jim. Make them understand. Promise."

"I promise. I will tell them exactly what you said."

She looked directly into my eyes. "Thank you for being my mom. I love you."

I held her close, then sat beside her. For the rest of the night neither of us moved.

The next morning Tom arrived about eleven. He took Karen's hand and began talking to her. I left the room to let them be together. Five minutes later, he joined me in the hall looking sad and weary. He said, "You need to get away for an hour. Let's go have lunch."

I wanted to be with Karen when she made her transition, yet this was the right time to tell Tom what she had said. I sent her a silent message to hold on while I kept my promise.

In the hospital cafeteria, Tom put catsup on his hamburger. I stared at my soup. I said, "She woke up last night and talked to me."

Before he could react, I described what had happened and told him every word Karen had said. I finished with, "She wants you to understand that she can't bear the thought of living as a vegetable, unable to think."

He said, "Of course I understand." I heard the anger in his voice and knew it wasn't directed at Karen or at me but at the destructive disease.

"Let's go back up," he said. "I'm not hungry."

The burger and soup sat on the table uneaten, surely a common sight in hospital cafeterias where people often hear bad news.

Back in Karen's room, a nurse was taking her pulse. She said, "We called Dr. Irwin. He's on his way. Do you still want us to do nothing, to let her go?"

Neither Tom nor I spoke for a moment, then he said, "It is her wish."

I breathed a sigh of relief. He had accepted Karen's desire, and I had kept my promise. I said, "Please, let us be alone with her."

Tom stayed only a minute. "I don't think I can be here," he said. "I'll wait outside."

I held Karen's hand. She didn't move, but a moment later I saw a fog-like substance rise from the top of her head and float toward the ceiling. I leaned over and kissed her on the forehead. "Good-bye," I whispered.

I had been privileged to see Karen emerge into her new life.

Later, Karen described her crossing in the writing: "I drifted in and out of consciousness. Occasionally a look on Mom's face jarred me. Dr. Irwin seemed overly concerned.

"Again and again my parents urged me to fight, reminding me we were The Three Musketeers and would always stick together. This took me back to my childhood, not just in memory but in some real way. During this period I floated back and forth between childhood and the present. Several times I clearly saw my Granddad who had passed on, but always it was connected with childhood and it seemed normal.

"I entered another world, the pain left, and I could rest. There I floated in a vast ocean of love and peace. I no longer felt concerned with my former problems. I was at one with the universe."

Tom and I sat with Dr. Irwin in a private office at the hospital. He talked about Karen as though she were his daughter. "I try not to become attached to my patients because it's too hard to see them die. But Karen was different. She was such a beautiful person." He wiped away the tears with his hand. He wasn't just trying to make us feel better.

He said, "She was funny. She teased me about being balder than she was. And she was bright too."

He looked at each of us in turn. "You know the disease was destroying her brain, and she wouldn't have wanted to live that way."

He deserved to know what she had told me. I said, "She woke from her coma last night for a short time. We talked."

"That happens," he agreed.

"She told me it was time for her to go on because she had lost her power to think. She said she couldn't bear to live without thinking, without intelligence."

He smiled. "Thank you for telling me."

As Tom and I drove home, the sun finally shone after days of rain. Snow glistened on the mountains above our home.
"Karen loved a day like this," I said.

He didn't answer. He had called Jim at school and asked him to meet us at our house. Tom asked, "What shall we say to Jim?"

"I will tell him what she said last night."

He looked hesitant, so I said, "Tom, there is no easy way. We all have to accept what has happened."

A little later, Jim came through the door—six feet, two inches tall, dark hair, handsome, quiet and resolute. As Karen once said, ". . . like the hero in a romance novel." When I saw him I remembered they had originally planned to be married in two days. Fortunately Jim seemed not to remember that.

*Amber–Karen's favorite dog–
a stubborn, affectionate dachshund*

Karen (age 14-½)

*Karen and Jim
eating popsicles
in summer 1968,
before illness*

*Karen, Nov. 1967 —
as bridesmaid at
wedding of friend
Carole*

*Jeanne and Karen,
during Karen's
illness, holding
Siamese twin dolls*

*Karen
on crutches,
Sept. 1970*

Karen and Jim,
1970–Karen
wearing wig

Jeanne and Tom,
1970–
about the time
"Always, Karen"
was published

7

C H A P T E R

NORMALLY WE WOULD ALL have returned to our jobs after the funeral, but the school Christmas break had begun. Just one year earlier Karen's illness had started. I thought perhaps the same people should all be together again. I suggested we take a trip to visit Gram in Palo Alto. Tom agreed. Jim decided to stay at home with his family for Christmas.

Jim and Tom and I comforted one another over the next few days. Jim stayed with us, helped with the phone calls to friends and relatives, participated in the final arrangements for our girl. We decided on cremation, burial in the ocean near Newport Beach, and a memorial time when her friends would remember her, each privately. We wanted no funeral service. That worked well for the three of us.

Tom and I said little as we drove the five hundred miles north. We held hands across the car seat, something we had never done before.

Seven hours from home, Tom maneuvered the car through the freeway traffic above Salinas. He said, "I wish I had some way to talk to Karen and be sure she's all right. I believe a loving girl like Karen will not go to any terrible place, but I'd like to know for sure."

"Me too." I said, "but how?"

"I know it sounds crazy, but we might try to locate a psychic."

I stared at him. I had read some psychic books, but when I had told Tom about them, he had shown little interest. I asked, "If a psychic did claim to locate Karen, would you believe it?"

He drove several miles before answering. Finally he said,

"Didn't you read about one who gave some kind of *evidence* from the person who had died? I think I could believe if that evidence was clearly from Karen."

I realized I was probably more skeptical than Tom. "That kind of information must be pretty rare. Where would we find such a skilled psychic?"

He let go of my hand. "I don't know." He sounded angry. "You're the one who reads that stuff. Where would you look?"

I almost yelled back at him, then stopped myself. He needed reassurance.

I tried to think of a reasonable answer. "When we get home we might try in Los Angeles. We could look for a bookstore that specializes in psychic books. They might give us a name. Or we could look in the phone book for a spiritualist church."

He took my hand again. "Sounds good. Maybe we could try in San Francisco and not wait until we get back to Los Angeles. We don't have to be in Palo Alto with the relatives on any special day."

Even though I was the one interested in the subject, I found it bizarre that two intelligent college professors would actually make such a weird search. Yet for Tom's sake, I was willing to try.

On December 22, we arrived in San Francisco to look for a person who could put us in touch with Karen. We had terrible luck there, almost as if we were supposed to fail. In fact, our adventure in finding a psychic became ridiculous. Each encounter was more ludicrous than the previous.

We found a metaphysical bookstore. From them we got the names of possible people to see. We called one woman and made an appointment for the next morning. She came to the door of her apartment wearing a robe, slippers, and a surgical mask.

She explained. "I lost my false teeth and didn't want anyone to see me without them."

Bizarre. When we told her we wanted to contact our dead daughter, she said she only read Tarot cards.

We could hardly contain ourselves. Despite our sorrow, on the way to the car we burst out laughing.

Next we went to a tiny shop. The entry was so crowded with Christian gift items and books that we had to move single file and turn sideways to get through. The woman who ran the store also mended clothing and told fortunes by reading palms. When she heard what we wanted, she readily agreed. "I contacted Moses only last week," she said. That, and her demand of a hundred dollar fee, sent us out the door as fast as the crowded aisle would permit.

Last we went to a Spiritualist church. The neighborhood was run down and spooky. About ten people sat in a dingy, unpainted room. They sang a few hymns, then one woman gave "spirit readings." She went around the circle of people and told each one what Aunt Suzy or Grandpa John had to say. The messages from the dead gave promises of making the person rich. When the psychic finally got to us, she named several people who were supposed to be our dead relatives. We didn't know a Maria, a Julian, or an Abraham. No one named Karen said a word.

That day in San Francisco, we learned that good psychics are rare.

After spending two days with Gram and my sister's family, we left for home on Christmas day. We drove silently, holding hands on the seat for comfort.

About two o'clock we came near Santa Barbara. I said, "I've been thinking about the book called *The Other Side* that I read last summer. The author, Bishop Pike, saw a medium in Santa Barbara who put Pike in touch with his dead son. But I don't remember the psychic's name."

Our search to find this man worked like magic—or as if someone named Karen was guiding us. We had two choices. We could wait until we got home, find my copy of Bishop Pike's book, and write or phone for an appointment. Or . . .

I said, "Maybe we could find a copy of *The Other Side* in a bookstore."

"No bookstore's open on Christmas day," Tom answered.

"Maybe a drug store?"

We found a Thrifty open and Tom looked on the rack of paperback books. He gave up and came back to the car.

"Give it one more try," I said. "Look behind books." I had no idea why I said that.

He tried and there was *The Other Side*. He bought it and opened it on the way back to the car. On the very page he chose was the name George Daisley of Santa Barbara.

Incredible.

"He's probably not in the phone book," said Tom.

But Daisley was listed. We knew it was rude to phone on Christmas day, but we did it anyway. Tom said to the very British voice that answered, "We have lost our daughter and would like to try to contact her."

"I have appointments for six months ahead," said Mr. Daisley.

Tom started to ask if we could set one up when the voice came on the phone again. "Just a minute. The spirits tell me I must see you immediately. Let me make a phone call and see if I can rearrange an appointment. Call me back in twenty minutes."

We waited for what seemed like hours and called back. "Can you come at ten tomorrow morning?"

Of course we could. We checked into a hotel and waited.

8

CHAPTER

TOM AND I had mixed emotions about seeing Reverend George Daisley. We were so sad and so anxious to reach Karen that we were very tense. If someone claimed to be Karen, how could we be sure it really was she?

"We must be sure to give Daisley no clues. Say as little as possible," Tom reminded me.

I agreed. "But if he's right about something, we should tell him so. Bishop Pike said that a sitting works better if you let the medium know when he is correct."

We had called Daisley at three on Christmas afternoon. He could not possibly have learned anything about us by ten the next morning. Any evidence he produced might possibly be explained away as telepathy from our minds. However, information came through in later sittings which we had not known and which we had to check with others for authenticity.

Karen's first personal message brought both tears and smiles to our faces. She picked the perfect way to convince us when she said, "I want you to know I still love you. We were The Three Musketeers, and we still are. We will still stick together."

We were stunned. Had that been the only message she got through, we would be forever grateful and certain of her continued life. But the evidence mounted for the next hour.

When we had arrived that morning, we were greeted by a tanned, carefully groomed gentleman. His British accent was charming, and he made us feel comfortable by talking about himself. He is a very religious man who has, for forty years, dedicated his life to God and to helping people who have lost their loved ones.

He explained to us how, through clairvoyance and clairaudience, he can see and hear the people who have died. He can describe them and repeat what they say. He isn't peculiar; he doesn't go into a trance; he sits alert in a chair and reports what he sees and hears. He handed Tom a tablet and suggested he take notes.

Next, he described Karen as sitting between us on the couch. He said, "She says to you," he pointed at Tom, "You're still the best dad in the whole world."

That was our second direct hit. She had told Tom that again and again, especially during the past year.

She went on, "I'm adjusting. Many wonderful people are here with me, helping. Don't wonder if I'm lost. I'm not. It's just as though I stepped into another room ahead of you." That was exactly why Tom had wanted to talk to her, to be sure she wasn't lost.

The sitting, we observed, developed a pattern fully as if it had been planned. Karen gave specific evidence followed by a message of reassurance. The evidence was of varying degrees of importance, sometimes showing her sense of humor. At the end we counted thirty-five direct hits.

Her next statement again made us gasp. "Thank you, Dad, for the single red roses. They were a symbol of love between us." She had remembered his trademark and was able to say it through another person who couldn't have known about the flowers Tom had given her during each hospital stay.

She struggled a little with the next message. It came through in two parts, like this: "Soon there will be a birthday, and I will be there." A little later, "My birthday is January 12. Please celebrate as we had planned, and give me a single red rose as a gift. Please be happy, for I will be." Getting the actual date right was remarkable. (Of course on her birthday we gave her the red rose and went out for dinner at her favorite restaurant to celebrate. We weren't as happy as she would have liked. It was too soon for that.)

"I come to you consolingly," she continued. "I want you to go away happy, and remember there will never be a day when I will not be with you often."

Suddenly George Daisley was squirming delightedly in his chair. "She's laughing and putting on false hair, and she says. "Mom, you and I talked a great deal about wigs. This was recent."

We laughed too. "Talked a great deal" was an understatement. Through all those months of chemotherapy and thinning hair, we talked daily about wigs.

"Your mother is still living, isn't she?" Daisley said this to me. Of course she is Karen's Gram. "Get in touch with both your mothers. Tell them how much she loves them. And tell Gram thanks for making this possible."

This requires an explanation. When we had visited Gram several days earlier, she mentioned knowing Diane Pike, Bishop Pike's wife. That had made me remember his book and think about trying to locate his medium.

Karen never stopped for a moment. "I have three coins that were special to me. Mom knows where they are. Keep them to remember me by." The number three was what made this correct. Reverend Daisley might have guessed that Karen had a coin collection, but that wasn't it. She meant, of course, the three Chinese coins that she used when she told fortunes with the *I Ching*. She kept the coins in the mouth of a ceramic frog near her bed, and I knew this, but Tom didn't.

Later we had two of these coins made into most unusual rings with her birthstone, a garnet, in the center. We always wear them. The third coin we glued on a wooden letter *K* and hung it over the front door of the house for protection. I guess we are just as superstitious as Karen admitted she was.

Later Daisley said, "She keeps saying the name Karen." It seemed that he didn't realize it was her name until she added, "Do you remember at one time I hated my name and tried to change the spelling from an *e* to a *y*? Maybe you let me get away with things like that because I was an only child."

Daisley next mentioned that he was noticing her clothes. "She is casual and stylish at the same time." He followed up on this in another sitting when we returned for more messages from Karen by saying, "She's saying something about noses." We were startled to see him stroke downward from the bridge to the tip of his own nose with his forefinger, then tilt his head back as he moved the finger upward across his nostrils. The haughty gesture was so exactly like the one Karen used constantly after her nose surgery that we laughed. With the demonstration, Karen and Daisley had communicated perfectly.

Reverend Daisley said to me, "She says you have her watch in her purse." He pointed to Tom, "And you have her picture in your wallet." Were these good guesses? Perhaps. But I did have the watch and I had been sad the whole trip because I didn't have a picture of Karen. Tom had the only one. About the watch, she said, "It isn't running right," (which is why I wasn't wearing it) "so get it repaired and wear it." I did.

Finally, Karen joked, "If you won't hold hands in the car, I'll sit between you on the way home." This meant she had been with us on the trip, because we had never before held hands as we drove. Karen obviously had a new body that we couldn't see, but just because it was invisible didn't mean it was comfortable for her to sit on a solid object like a hand. Something to think about.

Another message told us she knew about recent events. "When I saw you planned to cremate my body, I was horrified. But," she added, "cremation was better for me. Either cremation or burial is all right." Would she rather have been buried? We worried. In a later sitting she said again that she was not harmed by cremation.

Not all of the messages came from Karen. My father spoke and said that he was sorry he had not been close to me as an adult. "I'm sorry I didn't treat you better. I would do better as a dad now." My father had physically abused me when I was a child.

Tom's father said, "I was surprised at how many people disapproved of the way I died. I wish people could be more tolerant." Tom's father had been ill and had taken his own life. He was surely referring to that.

Tom and I had been so sad at losing Karen that in the days

since she died, we had talked about suicide ourselves. She admonished us through George Daisley. "You are not to take your lives by your own hand."

That day Karen had convinced us that she still lived and continued to be a part of our lives. As she said it, "I'm more alive than ever."

9

C H A P T E R

OF COURSE we had several more visits with Karen and Reverend Daisley. She often mentioned recent events right away.

Soon after the first sitting, Jim's old car broke down as it had many times. He had no way to get to and from Chapman University except by a long bus ride. We decided to give him Karen's red Toyota. At the next sitting, she said, "I had a small red car. You are welcome to it." The *you* obviously referred to Jim.

In later sittings she talked about her many animals. She started with one of the least important when she said, "Look for a picture of me when I was little on a pony at the zoo." We couldn't remember such a picture taken at the Los Angeles zoo. We looked through the photo albums and found one of her taken at the San Francisco zoo. We had forgotten that.

"And speaking of animals," she said, "the monkeys really messed up our house. I was mad when they used the hose to capture one of them."

Tom looked at me in doubt.

I laughed. "Surely you remember the two monkeys in Perris when Karen was about three. Karen and I trapped one on the porch and the police turned the fire hose on the other to catch him."

Tom finally remembered, but that evidence meant far more to me than to him. After all, I was the one who had scrubbed the monkey paw prints off the walls and ceilings.

Karen followed that up with "Do you remember the times we went to the zoo and watched the chimpanzee who spit water at people?" Tom did remember that one without help.

"Dogs were the best," she said. "I had a whole gang of them. Amber got old and gray. But the other one is the problem."

The "other one" was Mandy, one of Amber's puppies. Because she was the runt of the litter, she ate more than the rest. She nursed so often that she had a round, fat stomach. We named her Mandolin, after the round, fat musical instrument, and called her Mandy.

After Karen died, Mandy did an odd thing. She would sit for long periods of time staring into Karen's room. The room could be lighted or dark. We became convinced that perhaps she could see Karen occasionally.

At one sitting Karen said, "One of my dogs sees me and hears me call."

Both Amber and Mandy seemed to miss Karen. Tom and I wondered aloud several times whether she might like us to let her dogs join her. If this would make her life happier on the other side, we would send them on. Karen surely heard us talking, for in the next sitting she said, "Do not destroy the dogs. Let them live out their natural lives."

After Amber died from kidney failure and joined Karen, Mandy turned into a freak, a psycho. She *saw* Karen, and perhaps Amber also, even more often. Obviously she was lonely, for she howled constantly and disturbed the neighbors. She tried many times to chew through a sheet of plywood we used to keep her penned up when we were away from home. We worried that she might choke on the splinters.

Finally we talked aloud to Karen about Mandy. "Do you think we should send Mandy to be with you now? Can you tell us through George?" as we called Daisley by this time.

Karen didn't wait for us to schedule another sitting. She had George invite us to meet some friends of his. We arrived early and he gave us a sitting while we waited. Immediately Karen said, "It's time now to send the little dog across. She should join me. The time has come to free her from her psychological problems."

We shouted with delight. Not only did we have permission to free the poor animal from her misery here, but Karen's statement about psychological problems was exactly right, and we had never told George what was wrong with her. Surely he would have thought the animal was physically ill.

The next morning at home, Tom looked sadly at Mandy and said, "I know Karen said it's all right, but I just can't have her put to sleep. Maybe in a day or two."

A week passed, and Mandy was still howling and chewing the barricade. Then George called again. He told Tom, "Karen has been after me all day to give you a message. I told her I would write, but she said I must phone."

"What is it?"

"She says you have been stalling. Each day you put off sending her dog to her, and she's waiting to receive the animal. She says it's the proper time."

Mandy went to join Karen the next morning and we know both are happy.

Closely related to this idea of the proper time for death, especially for animals, Karen said one of her jobs was helping animals across. "They are bewildered when they arrive, and I help them find themselves." She added, "I like that job. If I were back on earth, I would not eat meat."

Karen had become a kind of veterinarian after all.

"The same day Karen said she would not eat meat, Tom and I went out for dinner and ordered prime rib. As I took my first bite, I remembered.

Tom laughed. "Don't worry about it. Karen's sitting beside you with the cow, explaining what a barbarian you are." In spite of my laughter, I ate only the vegetables.

Karen mentioned other dogs:

"I used to marry the dogs to each other.

"Dad and I took care of the strays, but he usually got the credit.

"Amber almost came across before her time when she had the surgery." Amber had had a tumor the size of a grapefruit removed while Karen was still alive.

Once during a sitting, Daisley looked startled. "My that's a gorgeous horse she's brought here." It was probably one of

Karen's favorites that she had ridden, but George doubtless worried that the horse would ruin his carpet, and who could blame him?

Karen gave me a poignant reminder of another creature. "A yellow butterfly became my friend. I held her on my finger and talked to her."

Karen was still the perfect only child who could entertain herself, and me.

Karen told us that it is especially difficult to give dates through a medium. Numbers are troublesome because they must be so precise. This was why we were happy when she had said she had *three* special coins.

Several times she gave exact dates, and I could imagine her jumping with joy when George heard them correctly.

She said, "There's a birthday coming on March 22. Please celebrate."

We couldn't remember a birthday on that date until several days later. Gram asked how old Amber was, and then we knew. March 22 was Amber's birthday, and Karen had impressed Gram to ask the question so we would remember.

Another time she told us, "June 24 is on my mind. There is an anniversary I want you to remember." This time we knew what she meant, for it was in June that she had her nose surgery. However, Tom and I both thought it had taken place much earlier in the month. Finally I phoned the doctor's office. Karen was right—June 24.

She mentioned that my birthday is early in November. She surely would have expressed her disgust at not getting the exact day.

Getting names and titles exact can be equally difficult. In one instance, Karen gave the exact title of a book we had just purchased. After our first sitting with George, we had started to read in the psychic field. We haunted used bookstores to locate copies of such books. Karen spoke of this. "You recently bought a book called *The New Revelation* by Arthur Conan Doyle. Read it." The message provided more evidence that Karen was still participating in our lives. And Doyle's book, when we read it, amplified much that we were beginning to learn about psychic communication.

Karen mentioned two of her girlfriends by name. "I go see Jerol and her baby sometimes."

And she said, "You have a picture of me as a bridesmaid at Carole's wedding."

Other specific names came through as well. Usually the individual was someone we knew who had passed on and was simply saying hello. My maternal grandfather identified both his relationship to me and his name, Charles. Tom's father gave his name as Edward. Two individuals said they were Tom's grandfather and uncle and that Tom was named for them. Tom was indeed named Thomas for his grandfather and Manson for an uncle.

Most spectacular of all, two unusual names came through perfectly. A man identified himself as Rex Wignall. He said he had worked with Tom at Chaffey College and added that he had died in an auto crash. Dr. Wignall, a Chaffey administrator, had indeed died in an accident on the German Autobahn.

A close friend who died ten years before Karen gave her name as Sarah Gant, then said, "You of all people should never have worried about Karen over here." This remark was so typical, we could almost hear her say it. Later we learned she became Karen's special guide in her new world.

Knowing Karen's urge to get good grades, Tom had once teased her by saying that Chaffey College might be harder than she thought. He bet her one hundred dollars that she couldn't get a perfect 4.0 grade point average one semester. Karen won that bet easily. She wouldn't even take the next bet. He told her he would give her another hundred dollars if she would select one subject and get a C in that course. She couldn't stand the thought of a C on her record.

During her last year and her illness, she often said that she wasn't getting A's any more. We thought about this when Granddad said, "It would be appropriate to tell you that Karen gets all A's over here. She didn't always there, and especially that last year."

She added, "I had to quit school before I could finish, but I will continue my schooling here, for I know it will please you."

A series of messages came through in different sittings that had to do with holidays in her childhood and the people she knew then. If you have read carefully, you won't need me to remind you what they mean.

"My birthdays were the best because of you, Mom. It always rained, but the church basement kept the kids busy. We played there.

"There's a picture of me in a ballet costume." The picture is with her cousin Janet at a family Christmas in Palo Alto.

Two messages came through about Beany. "Remember the gingerbread houses? Beany took them home and kept them." Karen and I had created elaborate gingerbread houses every Christmas. When we tired of them about Easter, Beany took them home with him for the next Christmas.

She also said, "Beany was sure scared by the organ. He never went upstairs in the church again."

She mentioned a "tooth that didn't grow right." She had worn braces for three years, but after they were removed, one front tooth re-twisted slightly. We urged her to return to the braces for a while longer, but she always refused and joked that everyone should have some slight imperfection.

She talked about her attempts at acting. "I'd like to be in plays over here. Remember I used to be in amateur theatricals there? I saw you looking at the Shakespeare books the other day," she continued. "There wasn't room on the shelf, and you tried to decide what to do with them." The set of books she referred to was an inexpensive paperback set of Shakespeare's plays. We had to do something about overflowing bookshelves. I tried to give the books to Jim. He had no interest in Shakespeare and graciously refused.

Once she said, "I'm very pleased with my legs now. Remember how much I complained about crutches?" At that point George had no idea Karen had used crutches.

Karen gave very few messages on the subject of her illness, and this surprised me at first. After twelve months of illness and pain, I had supposed she would, but apparently it seemed unimportant in her new life. However, once she said, "We were like Siamese twins, Mom, like the dolls."

The accuracy and the amount of evidence from Karen was astounding. In our reading of psychic material we have yet to discover any literature that has a more impressive collection of factual evidence than Karen's communication through George Daisley.

Anyone who has lost a loved one can imagine how important each bit of documentation is in establishing the nearness of that person. The most personal and trivial remarks accomplish this especially. For us, the conviction of Karen's presence was established in our first sitting, but every additional proof gave us renewed joy.

The notes Tom took during the sittings were soon indecipherable if we didn't transcribe them, so we used a tape recorder to do this. We not only clarified the notes but also discussed the exact wording of messages before these faded from our memories. Karen said, "I love to watch and listen after the sittings when you tape record the notes and talk over what I said."

I had not told George about the automatic writing, so when Karen said, "Someone is doing automatic writing. You're doing it the right way. Keep it up. It's important," I was thrilled. This came as I was about to give up, convinced that my unconscious was working overtime.

Sometimes Karen's personality came through in the comments of others on her side. In a discussion of her very human impatience and anger, my father once told us that when Karen had trouble getting a message through in the sittings she did everything but shout profanities. How polite of him. I'm sure our girl does shout profanities.

Tom's father added to this. "You must remember that she hasn't sprouted wings yet," he reminded us. "She can still get mad."

In the automatic writing, Karen had told of her depression during her illness. She confirmed this in the sittings. Then she said, "My equilibrium is being re-established and I am fine. I'm sorry about some things there on earth. I caused you worry, but even as I would think of asking you to forgive me, I know that you have, and it doesn't bother me anymore."

Eventually Tom and I stopped our visits with Karen through George. We knew she continued to live. She had proved over and over that she was still with us. Of course we still missed her, but we no longer needed constant contact.

One day at home, however, Karen gave a dramatic sign that she was with us. I had finally found the courage to go through her things. Of course I kept many items in the house. Jim took some of her books, her tapes, and other personal items. I stored some in her trunk in the garage.

About five years after she died, I spent a sentimental hour going through that trunk. I turned the pages of the scrapbook she had kept through high school: notes from friends, newspaper clippings, pictures, and the prom corsage. The ribbons were faded and the dried flower crumbled nearly to dust. It fell out of the book onto the garage floor.

I picked it up. It seemed too pathetic to keep, so I started to toss it in the nearby trash barrel.

Before I could drop it, three thunderous bangs sounded on the garage wall beside me. I quickly put the skeleton of a past romantic moment back in the book and sat down on a stool, shaken.

Tom ran out of the house. "Are you all right? What was that noise?"

I took a deep breath. "Karen, I think." I showed him the corsage and explained. "She definitely did not want me to throw it away."

He didn't quite believe me. He searched around all sides of the garage for some object—a ball? a rock?—that might have hit. He even got out a ladder and climbed up to check the roof. Nothing. At least his antics had made me see the funny side of Karen's protest.

"Do it again," he said.

"What?"

"Start to throw it in the trash."

I hesitated and then made the gesture.

One bang this time. I laughed. One was enough.

PART TWO

Karen's Life Continued

10

CHAPTER

THE PEN IN MY HAND moved rapidly and smoothly. After two months of automatic writing, Karen and I had become efficient. I was sufficiently confident that the writing was accurate and that I no longer needed to maintain the double consciousness. I could pay attention to what she said and ask questions. Until then she had used the writing to remind me of the stories about her that she wanted me to tell.

One day she said, "I want to describe what happened when I came across to this side. It will give me an opportunity to explain the sort of thing that happens to many people who come across."

"Are you sure I can get it right?" I asked.

"I can correct you."

I knew that. Whenever Karen took over the pen, I felt a tingling in my hand and arm. When I sometimes wrote words she did not intend, the tingling stopped and the pen refused to move. On one occasion, the pen had dropped to the table as she seemed to force it out of my hand.

"Listen to the story of my first birthday here," she wrote. "Mom, the night after you and I talked and you gave me permission to go on, I slept. Then I was out of bed, walking normally and feeling fabulous. People surrounded me, some I knew from the past and others I had never met. They seemed to be having a party, and I was the guest of honor. They greeted me with 'Happy Birthday.'

"Granddad was there. I hadn't seen him for eight years, but he looked the same. You know, Mom, how his iron-gray hair stuck straight up above his high forehead and made him look perpetually surprised. His matching iron-gray suit looked exactly like the one I had last seen him wear."

I smiled. "His new suits always looked just like the old ones," I said aloud.

The pen made a little squiggle, a movement that often seemed to come at a moment when Karen would normally laugh or chuckle. "Didn't they though?" she said, "As a child I was convinced he slept in a gray suit, white shirt and blue tie. When he hugged me the day I came across, he smelled like gray wool and the maple-flavored pipe tobacco he always carried in the pouch in his inside breast pocket."

She continued telling about her crossing. "A woman standing next to Granddad said, 'Remember me?'"

"Mom, it was Sarah Gant. She looked the same as before. We talked about the Saturday night enchilada dinners at her house and the candy jar filled with treats for me to choose from. And Laddie was with her; he jumped on me and licked my face."

Laddie had been the Gants' collie. After the enchilada dinners Karen would sit on a huge leather footstool with Laddie beside her and watch television.

"Other people greeted me," Karen wrote. "They distracted me for a while, but then a wave of sadness washed over me. I wanted to know about you and Dad and Jim."

"Sarah read my thoughts. 'Karen, I've known Jeanne and Tom for years. Your parents will miss you terribly, but they are receptive. You will find a way to talk to them. Not everyone can do that, but you can. And they will take care of your love, Jim.'

"She took my hand and performed some small magic that temporarily erased my sadness. For the next hour I danced on my new perfect leg at my birthday party—the party that welcomed me to my new world."

The pen moved ponderously as it wrote the next words.

"Many times in the next days I would think: *Dying is easy. Separation is the hard part.*"

❀ ❀ ❀

82

The next day my hand tingled again and Karen took over. She wrote, "I made my transition easily. Some people have to be put to sleep until they can be treated to help them make the adjustment. For two reasons, I didn't have to wait. The depression, anxiety and darkness I had experienced during my illness prepared me. Also, you and Dad released me. Your willingness to let me go gave me a head start here.

"I'm glad," I said aloud. "Were you happy? Sad? Angry?"

"All of that and more. I was happy. Within twenty-four hours I acclimated to my new world and loved it. Such relief and freedom after a year of pain and crutches, to be able to walk normally and feel great. I felt better than I had ever felt on earth. I was happy, and baffled too."

"Why?"

"Because everyone seemed the same. Granddad. Sarah. Except for feeling good, I was the same Karen. I asked Sarah how this could be Heaven or Hell when everything was so nearly the same as before."

"What did she say?"

"She said that it's neither. It's all one 'place.' Then she brought me fully into my new world. One minute I saw her as the former Sarah; the next instant she glowed with light and color."

"How did she accomplish that magic?" I asked.

"She raised my frequency so that I moved into my new body."

The pen stalled for a minute, then Karen wrote. "One of the first requests I made was to see you and Dad and Jim. Of course you were grieving. That made me sad and angry. I said to Sarah, 'How unfair to have to die so young: ahead of Mom and Dad and without marrying Jim.' A part of me wanted to blow up the universe."

"You grieve too?" I asked.

"Our personal loss is as deep as yours. In addition, your grief pulls us back. Some people can't handle it. If their bereavement is too devastating, either because of their own personalities or because those left behind are too demanding, they must remain unconscious for a longer period."

"But you said you were angry as well. Did you make any attempt to 'blow up the universe?'" I asked.

"I'm too civilized for that. After all, my mother raised me to behave properly."

I could picture Karen giving a rueful smile.

"I did have a terrible moment two days after I arrived," she said, "when I realized that it should have been my wedding day. I was devastated. I looked for Jim and saw that he hadn't remembered yet. Thank God for that."

"What other reactions did you have?"

The pen seemed to hesitate. "Well, shock. I thought you had made bizarre arrangements for my body. When I saw that you planned cremation, I yelled, 'How could you permanently destroy such a beautiful body. Stop it.'

"Sarah calmed me by saying, 'It doesn't matter. You won't need that tired old thing ever again. Besides, you will be more beautiful here.' She explained why cremation was good. It was often better for the person who had passed over to be rid of the body entirely. That eliminated the close attachment that some people feel for their old life. Once you disposed of my body so permanently, you freed me to start my new life," she said.

When I knew about Karen's dismay about cremation, I felt guilty. Her last words had comforted me. Still, I said, "I'm sorry that we upset you. It just seemed a cleaner, way of reaching closure."

She answered, "I was afraid that telling you would send you on a guilt trip. Don't let it. You did the right thing. Actually, you opened the way for me to think about how people on both sides handle death. And you opened the way for me to talk about it to our readers, so I'll say one more thing. Either method of disposal—burial or cremation—that returns the body to its natural components is good. 'Ashes to ashes, dust to dust' makes complete sense."

"I suppose if you were shocked at cremation, you were equally shocked that we had no funeral service."

I felt the pen squiggle as though she might be laughing. "I was beyond surprise by then. At first I pouted because I wouldn't have a funeral with relatives and friends, masses of flowers, a eulogy, and much weeping. But Mom, what you did was perfect. You set aside that specific time at 2:00 P.M. on December 19. When each friend took that time alone to think about me, pray for me, talk to me, I was overwhelmed with more love than I've never known before. It was so powerful that it became a garment I have worn with joy ever since. When I explain ThoughtForms to you, you will understand."

With those reassuring words, Karen stopped the writing for another day.

Several days later she wrote, "Grief is a strong natural emotion that some people literally wear. I could see it around you and Dad and Jim. I had to help, so I talked with Sarah.

"Sarah said,'Your parents are receptive people and can be guided; they can help Jim and others. You must not let their grief drag you down, and helping them is the best way to avoid this danger.'"

I protested. "I understand your needing to help, but I don't see how we could be expected not to grieve."

"Of course, everyone grieves for loved ones. Most people try to postpone it by finding something to do until some time has passed. I did that, and so did you. Jim went to his parents' house for Christmas, so he could absorb the love of his family. You went on your trip. I got busy.

"Sarah and others told me, 'Set yourself a goal, to make your presence so certain to your family that they will never doubt you are with them.' They suggested helping you locate a medium so I could prove my continued presence with you.

"Dad's need to find and protect me was greater than yours, so I impressed him with the idea of looking for a medium. You had read Bishop Pike's *The Other Side* only a few weeks before my last hospital stay. That made you remember Reverend Daisley. I sent you on that farcical search for psychics in San Francisco to set the scene for the success with Reverend Daisley."

"You did keep us amused."

She squiggled her laugh. "Some day Dad will realize that I got even for all the practical jokes he played on me over the years."

She continued, "A group of people here pitched in to train me for my upcoming debut as a medium from this side. At least a dozen participated and many more watched the sitting you had with Daisley. A clear contact with your side is an event here. They were hoping for that.

"An actual team of people on this side represented a variety of talents: the equivalent of nurses, teachers, mediums, guides, writers, thinkers, and technicians all participated."

I couldn't resist interrupting. "I think I understand the reasons for all those people, but I'm curious about the technicians. Are these the equivalent of people on my side who handle cameras and microphones?"

"In a way. Think about the technology you use for communication to transmit words, voices, and pictures. Electricity is the medium, the go-between. Your technicians manipulate electrical frequencies. On our side, we can transmit directly through thought; we don't need electricity. Our technicians directly manipulate the frequencies of the actual people, the mediums on both sides involved in the communication.

"Whether technicians work with a medium like Daisley for a sitting or work with you to help you receive this automatic writing, the method is the same. They control and protect your body; at the same time they raise the frequency of your mind."

"Frequency? Some kind of vibration? I didn't know I had a frequency."

"I suppose not, but you can figure out what it is." She paused. "A thinker just gave me a definition."

I pictured someone handing her a scrap of paper with a written definition for her to read. Later, when I learned more about their communication, I realized no one handed anyone anything. More likely someone directed a ThoughtForm her way.

She said, "Electrical frequency is the number of repetitions of unit time of a complete waveform, as of electric current. From that can you figure out what biological frequency is?"

I tried to oblige. "I suppose it's the number of repetitions or vibrations of unit time of . . .," I struggled, " . . . of a body?"

"Not bad. But forget the idea of vibration. That's reducing frequency to tuning forks. What I'm after is closer to energy: vigor or power in action; the capacity for action or accomplishment. Relate that to humans."

"Being," I said almost without thinking.

"Good for you. What do you mean by being?"

"An inward feeling of self. My individual consciousness."

"Right. And your being or consciousness resides in a body. So does mine. Your being (and mine) is the real you, the seed of self. Frequency is the individual consciousness in motion. Bodies are only the shells that consciousness inhabits."

I tried to follow her thought as she said, "Go back to the definition you struggled with: human frequency is the number of repetitions of unit time of a body. But since bodies contain consciousness and consciousness is the real self, the definition I will give now would be more accurate: *Frequency is the number of repetitions of unit time of an individual consciousness.*

"Mom, even though your individual consciousness is well-developed, it nonetheless lacks energy because it is hampered by the density of your world. It is obstructed. Its frequency must be raised for it to receive messages from me.

"Technicians do that. They step up the number of repetitions of unit time of your being, your consciousness. Later I can explain more clearly the method they use. Perhaps this will help. Just as on your side your technicians use electricity as a conduit, technicians here use thought projections. Because the body houses your consciousness, it must be kept safe and comfortable during the raising of your frequency. Our medics here do that."

The pen stopped for a moment, then resumed. "Your medics tell me you've had enough for today. See you later."

I graded a stack of student essays, so two days passed before Karen took over my pen again.

She said, "When that first sitting with Reverend Daisley was over, people here celebrated with our equivalent of back-slapping and hugging. We were jubilant about accomplishing our goal.

"That was when Sarah told me their real plan. 'This is only the beginning for you, Karen. You have a job to do—to contact as many people on earth plane as possible with the message of assurance about our lives.'

"I thought she was joking. This had to be a job for experts, not a rookie like me. 'I've only been here a few days. Why me?'

"Sarah grinned and said, 'Because you're an A student. Because this is the way angels earn their wings.'"

I stopped the pen and said aloud, "I can almost hear her saying that. I guess she meant it."

Karen said, "Sarah told me not to worry, that I wasn't alone. Many people before me have done this. I am only one of a chain of individuals chosen to serve the great purpose of evolution."

"Why you?" I asked.

"My question exactly. She said it was because of my talents and yours, Mom. They've observed that you and I have a close telepathic relationship. We're mental mediums. I can easily impress you with ideas."

I nodded. "What else did you learn?"

Karen said, "I wanted to know how we would get the message across, and she told me that you and I would write a book."

I had to have my say. "It seems they were pretty sure of me."

"They have their ways of working. They impressed you with the importance of the knowledge of continued life through a series of incidents. One was Gram. I tried to comfort her but with little success, so I had you write her about the sitting with Daisley. You were surprised at how readily she believed."

Karen continued, "You told a few friends about the sittings and were amazed that no one thought them weird. For example, Carole, my old high school buddy, dreaded to come see you, so she waited several weeks. When she finally did arrive and you told her about contact with me, she also became a believer. She talks to me aloud occasionally. And by the way, she's expecting a baby, a girl."

I was surprised. "She hasn't told me."

"You'll get an announcement."

Karen went on describing her efforts to convince me to write by working with Jim. "My biggest challenge was Jim. I wanted so to comfort him; he was inconsolable. The messages I sent through Reverend Daisley were for him as much as for you, and they helped, but not enough. [The beautiful letter of reassurance that Karen sent to Jim via me is reproduced at the end of this chapter so that others may find comfort in it too.]

"After Christmas he went back to school, so lonely. He came to talk to you and Dad about quitting school. I knew I had to get through to him some way. I tried and tried to make him hear me, but I couldn't. Finally I kicked him on the shin the way I had when we studied together. I could tell by his reaction he had felt it physically.

"It startled me too. I yelled at him. 'Are you a man or aren't you? I've invested too much of my life in you to let you give up now. If you don't finish school now, you'll never finish.'

"He rushed home to tell you what I'd said."

"I know," I told her. "He kept saying, 'She really kicked me; I felt it.' When we asked what he planned to do, he said, 'Stay in school, of course. She's really here. I can't let her down now.' "

I was curious. "How did you make him feel an actual physical kick?"

"A ThoughtForm. Be patient. I'll tell you about that soon."

Karen came back to her own agenda. "It took some doing on our part, but you finally started to write the book. Such a sentimental female you are," she teased me. "You wanted to wring tears from everyone. I had to wait until you became disgusted with the effort before I could get through, and then I had to sneak up on you. The doubts and anguish almost did us in, but how can I blame you?" She forgave me with her next sentence. "In your position I would probably have quit on the first day."

❀ ❀ ❀

My arm tingled more than usual. The pen picked up speed and seemed jubilant. "Sarah has become my personal guide. She is such a dear, so loving, and so wise. She has been helping me decide what jobs I want to do here."

The pen continued. "She tells me that the central reality of your world and mine is the evolution of consciousness. All beings are in evolution toward higher and higher levels of consciousness. Individual evolution functions on your side with little planned participation. However, when a person reaches a certain level of consciousness, usually here in my world, she or he begins to participate actively in aiding the progression of all evolution. Each individual consciousness should participate as her or his abilities and attributes dictate."

She continued, obviously excited. "My abilities incline me toward teaching and guidance. This makes me suitable to help with the project of this book. I have chosen other ways to serve here as well. I will teach at the university level, and guide young children who come across. I love this. I also plan to guide animals across, as a hobby."

My mother instinct took over. I questioned the wisdom of so many committments on Karen's part. "How can you possibly do all that?"

"We have twenty-four hours a day." Then she modified her statement. "It seems that way because time is not so restrictive for us as it is for you. We can use it more efficiently."

She quit writing at that point, leaving me intrigued about how they might manipulate time.

Karen wrote one special message through the automatic writing that was "both private and public."

"This is to Jim" she told me. "Just once in all my messages I must speak directly to him. But it is also for the world to read, for it is a kind of message so many here want desperately to send their dearest one."

Dear Jim,

Such a very long time we've been apart, yet not apart. For you it was often so lonely, frustrating, hopeless. You and I know the awful unfairness of separation. There was no time for our plans: our marriage, our family, our growing closer with the years. In a surge of love we reached for each other only to be swept apart as we barely touched.

But I'm always here, Jim, and you know that. You remember the first contact I made just two nights after our separation. You lay in our spare room trying to sleep, but no sleep would come. I longed so to help. And, Jim, I held you close just as you had held me during those long months just past. Again and again I said, "I'm here, darling. I still love you. I haven't gone anywhere, Jim; please listen. " And you heard! I could scarcely contain my joy when you rushed to tell my folks you felt my touch and knew I was there. That gave me courage to go on, too, for I was as bereft as you, yet for the first time I knew I could still contact you when I needed to. We've repeated this experience. As you well know, I am always just a need away.

Two years have passed. The awful ache and loneliness have lessened, and you have moved purposefully ahead. As hard as it was, you went on to finish school. You have fine goals ahead. And I do love you for that. And Jim, how you've matured. Are you aware how much? Few young men have your perception, your sensitivity. You have lifted yourself from the rigidity of physical obstructions. You have the porousness and fluidity of the spiritual.

Now before you sprout wings and I become unrecognizable as a sentimental jerk, I must add that I still want to kick you sometimes. You know when. Just remember we don't kick people we don't love.

Would you believe I'm different too? What would you most have liked to change about me? My vain perfection in grooming? My attempts to dominate? My insecurity about being loved? I'm sorry, but the old complaints would probably remain. Yet I, too, have matured.

This is so difficult to say, but we both know the truth and must face it. Jim, I must keep right on living in my new dimension. You must keep on living for a time in yours. Nothing remains static; we both will continue to change, to grow. So, for the last time let me say: Don't let me down, Jim. Acquire all the quantity you can. Live earth life to the fullest: work, serve, love. Jim, find someone to share that life with and make it rich. Marry. Have children. Life offers many loves, and we must treasure each one. This is the natural way, and I covet it for you because I love you so.

I, too, must move forward in the natural way for my dimension. My life will also include work, service, and love. Release me to this joyously. Want it for me because you love me.

Life is eternal. Love is eternal. Let ours give testimony to this truth.

Always,
Karen

11

C H A P T E R

"Think about this," Karen said. "I'm here. Right here."

So why was that news?. "I know," I answered. "This is our time for the automatic writing."

"You're not paying attention. I mean my world is right here. We live in the same world."

"Of course. I didn't think you'd gone to Mars."

"Then why do you look up when you talk to me?"

That stopped my sarcasm. I didn't look up. Or did I?

"It's a typical earth reflex," she said. "Almost everyone does it. When you think of the dead, when you speak to us, your eyes flick heavenward. But you're looking in the wrong place. I'm right here beside you. We live in the same world," she repeated.

A pause ensued while I thought about the perception she wanted to correct. At first the point seemed trivial. I had thought the fact that we could communicate was the important thing. Whether her "voice" came from heaven or beside me in my study seemed irrelevant, yet she wanted to discuss it.

I could feel her scribbled chuckle as she said, "I suppose I should be pleased that you don't look down. At least you assume I made it to heaven."

I ignored *her* smart-aleck remark and said, "I'll go along with you. Obviously this means something you want me to understand. You don't live in heaven. You live in my world somehow, but I don't see or hear you."

"Right. You and I live in the same world. The world you experience is a limited version of mine. Our worlds are concentric."

The writing stopped abruptly, then said, "Wrong word. Try again. Think about something else for a minute and let me take another stab at it."

I switched my attention to a new stack of student essays sitting on the corner of my desk and began reading the one on top. Pronoun agreement in the third sentence. Fragment in the fourth. That certainly distracted me.

The pen began to scribble on Karen's page just as I found a misspelled word.

"Our worlds are concurrent." My eyes returned to Karen's page as the pen wrote. "Yes! You got it."

She continued. "Concentric means having a common center. That's too visual. Our worlds are concurrent: happening at the same time; meeting at the same point. They inhabit the same 'space' and 'time.'"

I asked my question again. "Same space and time? So why can't I see and hear you?"

"Because of the limitation of your physical body. Because your spiritual body isn't sufficiently fine-tuned to permit it."

"Sounds like a great idea for a science fiction novel," I joked. "The main character learns to fine-tune her eyesight and see things no one else can see."

Karen refused to be diverted. "Here's the point. I live in the extended world, the real world. You live in a limited aspect of the extended world. You are limited by the restriction of your perception."

"So you can see or hear me any time you want?"

"Certainly. I modify my frequency when I want to be involved in your world. But our worlds have the same essential elements: trees, dogs, people—rainbows. I see them in their essence, their basic nature; you see them in their likeness, their reflection."

"And what does a tree look like in its essence?"

"You know. You saw their essence once years ago."

A picture flashed in my mind. We had lived in Perris, California. Karen was two. On a winter night I awoke about three in the morning unable to sleep but feeling euphoric. Despite the cold of the drafty old parsonage, I felt warm. I wandered in my nightgown and bare feet to the back porch. As I looked into the yard, every living thing seemed to glow from within. Auras of colored

94

light surrounded the trees. Strands of white light, like webs of thread, connected all of the vegetation and revealed its kinship.

I stared in awe.

Up the road beside the house walked an elderly man and his dog. They too glowed and the white strands connected them with one another, with the trees, with me. I saw my own aura around my outstretched hand. In that instant, I knew the interrelatedness of all living things.

"I was seeing your world?"

"You were seeing the extended world."

"How did I do that?"

"By raising your frequency. You remember at that time you were immersed in learning meditation techniques. You lifted yourself out of the density of your body. By practicing meditation, you had earned the momentary breakthrough into the extended universe."

"The world you see glows?"

"And more. Imagine your other senses involved as well. What sound would you expect to hear from a glowing tree?"

"Some sort of music. Tree music, or whispers perhaps."

"Close enough. What odor?"

"Depends on the tree. They smell different here, so I suppose they do there."

Karen waited for me to follow through on her thoughts. I complied.

"I suppose they also have taste and feel. And I suppose if the visual images of trees become more awe-inspiring on your side, so do the involvement of the other senses as well."

"Right," she agreed. "Everything is intensified, and that is one reason you don't normally experience the extended world. The intensity would overwhelm you. The full experience must wait until you are ready to leave your present body."

"So you have a new body. Do you glow like the man I saw on the road the night of my 'experience'?"

"I glow more, but what you saw gave you a glimpse."

I thought of a dozen questions.

Karen answered before I could voice any of them. "Hold on. I can't explain everything at once. Let me give you the ideas in a rational order.

"My thought for this day is that we have one world. You live in a restricted aspect of it; I, in an unlimited aspect. Our worlds are concurrent, inhabiting the same 'space' and 'time.' What you don't understand is how they function. Our problem is with language. We need some definitions."

"Such as?"

"Well, 'limited' and 'extended,' aren't accurate, for example. "Let's get at the idea this way. Today you have a bruise on your shin, and you don't remember how you got it. It happens to you all the time."

"I admit I'm clumsy. What's the message?"

"The message is that you bump into things. Not just you— everyone does. You do it with your bodies and, more disastrously, with your cars and other vehicles. You run into obstructions. Your solid world is obstructed."

"And yours isn't."

"Because our world is more fluid, it is unobstructed. The difference is in the density of the two. Our unobstructed world consists of much finer, lighter substance. This includes our bodies."

Those words reminded me. I had once read *The Unobstructed Universe* by Stewart Edward White.

Karen knew my thought. "That's right, Mom. Locate your copy of that book if you like, but please don't reread it for the moment. I want the message I am giving to come through my hand. Later you can refer to the book for confirmation.

I did look for my copy of White's book and couldn't locate it. By the time I found it in a box in the garage weeks later, Karen had written this chapter and the several more. I'm sure she deliberately prevented my finding the White book. When I did read it, she had already given me three major ideas: we live in the same world; consciousness is the main component of the entire universe; thought is the most important form of consciousness. This last idea became a major theme of the automatic writing and went far beyond anything in S.E. White's book.

She continued her current theme. "You see the same world we do, only less vividly. It's like the difference between radio and television. Hearing the news on your car radio informs you. Seeing it on television in color almost puts you on the scene."

Karen continued, "In my analogy the radio world is the equivalent of yours; the television world is the equivalent of seeing things as I do. One of the pleasurable differences about my world is not bumping into things."

I asked, "Aside from avoiding bruises, what's the big deal about that?"

"The big deal is that obstructions promote disease."

She had hinted at that in the sittings when she said she no longer hurt. "You don't have disease?" I asked.

"Not to the extent that you do. Consider the true sense of the word. Break it down: dis = absence of; ease = the condition of being without discomfort. Further meanings of "ease" include not only absence from physical pain, but also less worry, agitation, constraint, difficulty. In such an unobstructed world, consciousness can grow."

She stopped the pen. "Wrong word. Divert your attention and try again," she ordered.

This time I relaxed, closed my eyes, and tried to make my mind a blank while the pen wrote some more. "Consciousness can evolve."

The pen slid from my hand. I grabbed it back and it wrote one more sentence. "Consciousness is the central reality in both the obstructed and unobstructed worlds. The main purpose of the universe is the *evolution* of consciousness."

Two days later, the pen asked a question to get the writing restarted. "So, what do you know?"

"That you're here." I can be a good student.

"What else do you know—about yourself?"

"I suppose I know that I'm here too."

"Clever lady," Karen applauded. "You took a few philosophy classes in college. What did you learn?"

I parroted Descartes. *"Cogito ergo sum.* I think, therefore I am."

"Yea, Mom! You know that you exist as an 'I-Am.'"

I cooperated and followed up on the logic. "Even though I believe I perceive other people, other entities, I can't know *they* exist the way I know that *I* exist. Therefore, I can only *know* my own consciousness."

"That's it!" The pen seemed to shout. "Consciousness is the key word. What was the last thing I said to you the other day?"

I checked the writing to be sure I was accurate. I read aloud. " 'Consciousness is the central reality in both the obstructed and unobstructed worlds. The main purpose of the universe is the evolution of consciousness.' "

"Good. What does that suggest?"

"That my consciousness is evolving. And so is yours and your dad's and everyone's, I suppose."

"Good, again. Evolving how?"

That wasn't so easy. "I guess by gradually changing into a different and more complex and perhaps better form. But . . ."

I finally asked, "Is consciousness only human? Even though consciousness in humans implies self-awareness, isn't there another level of consciousness, perhaps simple awareness? A dog may not think about its own existence, but it has awareness at a level of sensing or perceiving. For all I know, so does a plant."

"Exactly. Consciousness comes in many degrees. Many of them below the level of self consciousness. Here's the key. Consciousness is any degree of awareness that can modify and change of its own accord."

I hesitated because my next thought seemed so farfetched. "That would seem to include entities as primitive as cells."

Karen answered, "It would indeed. Individual cells are self-perpetuating; in response to outside stimuli, they modify and change—evolve—of their own volition. They contain a physical mechanism that allows for modification to take place. They don't 'think' like the human mind, but they do function at their own level. The 'thought' produced by a cell is bred into it through DNA. Any modification in the genes, and ultimately in the cell, is pretty much automatic. Nonetheless, because genes respond to environmental stimuli and because they can modify, they are bits of consciousness in evolution."

She paused to let me absorb her definition of consciousness. I had a question. "If consciousness is any degree of awareness that can modify and change of its own accord, then is it possible that the most important form of consciousness is thought itself?"

For the moment, Karen didn't answer directly. She only said, "The key to understanding consciousness and evolution is thought."

12

C H A P T E R

"LISTEN!" Karen paused dramatically before she let the pen go on. "Thoughts are entities of consciousness."

"I remember that from reading the S.E. White book years ago," I told her. "But I believe it said 'Thoughts are things.' "

"I hoped you would remember. Now notice that in spite of your previous contact with that idea, I deliberately changed it. I got my message through. How's that for proving to you that I control our dialogue?"

"So the White book was wrong?"

"Not wrong. 'Things' is correct in that thoughts have form. They are *real*. But the word 'things' fails to pinpoint what kind of thing we are talking about—not inanimate things like a table or a car. A thought as an entity of consciousness has the component of awareness or being. Do you remember when we talked about frequency?"

I had memorized the definition. I said, "Frequency is the number of repetitions of unit time of individual consciousness."

"Show off," Karen laughed. "We said that each individual consciousness—whether plant, animal, or human—has a certain degree of frequency. Human consciousness has higher frequency than animal, animal higher than plant. Now here's today's challenge. What form of consciousness, do you suppose, has the highest frequency?"

"I would have said God, but I suppose you're suggesting it's thought."

" 'God' wouldn't be wrong," answered Karen, "but it's sort of begging the question. Consciousness is in evolution. In your world, human consciousness is the most fully evolved. What has it evolved to?"

"I suppose to a thinking consciousness."

"Right!"

I said aloud. "So thought is the highest form of consciousness?" I had a problem with that. "If I am a high form of consciousness, and I produce thought, then how is thought higher than I am?"

"Are you so sure that you produce thought?"

"I think I do. But you're suggesting that I don't."

Karen urged me on. "Turn the equation around. Perhaps you retrieve thought as well as produce it."

"You're probably right. I suppose I get most thoughts from outside myself, but where?"

"They can come from people in our world or from beings beyond us. This would explain discoveries in science and creative ideas in literature or art that sometimes happen simultaneously in various parts of your world. This was what Carl Jung called synchronicity. Those people are picking up extrasensory thoughts from beings beyond your world or from pools of ThoughtForms. (More on this later.) If the person receiving the thought is sufficiently advanced spiritually, the idea can even come from the essence of thought, or God. Great religious leaders and saints would fit into this category."

I put it into words. "Then the essence of thought, God, is the highest form of consciousness."

The pen wrote "You've got it!" across the entire page. "Of course God cannot be limited to thought, but the source of the highest form of thought is God."

I felt humble. "I suppose even my loftiest thoughts come from relatively low on the scale of consciousness."

"You're right. In your world, you seldom tap pure thought. You absorb even your most significant thoughts from entities in our world. You absorb thought at the level that your frequency can attract.

"Consciousness takes form. It is housed in a body. In either world, the body or form is a temporary arrestment of consciousness. When you are ready to move to another stage of life, you shed one body for another. You see only half of the change. You call it death. We see the entire change and call it continued life.

"One more thing. In your world the arrestment of consciousness in a form or body leaves it vulnerable to disease. Be aware of that. By your own efforts with ThoughtForms, you can learn to avoid and cure disease."

The pen stopped, then said, "The medics say you need rest. Lie down for five minutes then come back."

I fell asleep and returned an hour later.

"That's better," Karen wrote when I returned. "For accuracy we wanted you rested. It's time to summarize what we have told you in the last weeks. .

"1. We live in one universe. Our two aspects of that universe, our worlds, are concurrent. They inhabit the same space and time.

"2. Your world is obstructed; mine is unobstructed. You bump; I flow. Your bumping into obstructions causes disease and slows change; my fluidity allows for evolution.

"3. The central reality of both worlds is consciousness. Consciousness is any degree of awareness that can modify and change of its own accord. It exists in degrees: plant, animal, human. Other kinds exist: lower, such as cell, and higher, such as thought.

"4. All consciousness is in evolution, and the goal of individual consciousness should be to participate in the progression of evolution.

"5. All consciousness has frequency: the number of repetitions of unit time of individual entities of consciousness.

"6. The frequencies in either world are arrested in individual consciousness that is housed in body or form. Frequencies and their bodies or forms—arrestments—on your side are obstructed; frequencies and their arrestments on mine are unobstructed.

"7. Because consciousness is the one reality in the universe, the essence of all consciousness is thought, which at the lowest level is involuntary and at the level of humans is voluntary. Generally humans in your world produce thought that is received from my world or from the essence of thought.

"8. The highest form of consciousness is the essence of thought.

"9. At levels below the highest, consciousness absorbs thought. At all levels, consciousness also produces and transmits thought. The level of thought produced by an individual consciousness depends on the frequency of that consciousness.

"10. Because consciousness is in evolution, then the highest form of consciousness—the essence of thought or God—is in evolution. Because essence of thought, God, is the highest form of consciousness, it does not absorb thought from beyond itself. However, God does constantly evolve into a more complex form and, presumably, more advanced thought."

Finally Karen wrote, "We haven't discussed the last point. I write it only to draw the logical conclusion. Notice that I omitted one word from the usual definition of evolution, that an entity *gradually* changes into a more complex form. The omission is important. If time as you know it doesn't exist, then *gradual* is insignificant."

13

CHAPTER

"B*e careful* what you think," Karen warned. "It can take on a life of its own."

"Is this a new version of 'As a man thinketh in his heart, so is he'?" I asked.

My question took our conversation on an unexpected tangent that proved fruitless except that it revealed how Karen's team on the other side worked. I include it here for that insight.

The episode went this way. After my question I waited—then waited some more. The tingling in my arm subsided. Finally the pen wrote hesitantly, "The quotation should read, 'As he thinketh in his heart, so is he' (Proverbs 23:7)."

I was astonished. Karen had no such detailed knowledge of the Bible.

The pen wrote again with Karen's usual assurance. "Mom, that was Julia, one of the thinkers here. She's our Biblical expert and insists on accuracy."

"Then, thank you, Julia," I said aloud. "But does the quotation apply at all to what Karen is talking about?"

Karen wrote. "Julia says the sentence in the Bible refers to being cautious about trusting rulers who mislead, but that most people take it to have a more general meaning."

Another pause. For discussion?

Karen came back firmly with both the pen and the ideas under control.

"In a roundabout way your quotation gives me an opportunity to make a point. Thinking about something in one's heart suggests the person is keeping that thought a secret. However, you remember I said that thoughts are entities of consciousness. Entities do have form and are therefore difficult to conceal.

"And that brings me to ThoughtForms. In this regard I have two important messages: the importance of thought as *reality* and the problem of obstructed thought in your world."

She said, "The idea of thought as reality can be very practical."

I liked that. "Don't get me wrong," I told Karen. "I like your high-flown teachings, but I get a little weary of struggling with them. My hunch is that our readers will appreciate something useful. Are we going to get a 'how to' lesson?"

"Why not. Let's give it a title: *How to Make Petitionary Prayer Work.*"

Karen began her instruction. "Learning to create Thought-Forms can be practical in accomplishing a variety of goals: acquiring material objects, getting events to happen, influencing other minds. We're talking about getting the kinds of things you often pray for. The trouble is that when you pray, you tend to whimper 'please' or shout 'help' and then sit back and wait for a miracle. Make your pleas potent; learn to create ThoughtForms."

Karen's pen chuckled. "Now be patient a minute while I remind you that thoughts are entities of consciousness. All forms of consciousness are *born*. Therefore, a powerful thought must be born. Once another form of consciousness—a human—gives birth to a ThoughtForm, that new consciousness has life and the potential for activity. It can attract or repel.

"Suppose that without knowing how, you have been able to give birth to a powerful ThoughtForm. You send your infant out, directing it to another person through time and space. That person, depending on her receptivity, absorbs the Thought-Form and assimilates it. She can let it stop there or send it on to others.

"The further it moves through time and space, the more likelihood that your ThoughtForm will dissipate. However, the second person could add to its potency before sending it on. Thought-Forms often maintain life for a great period of time and travel over great distances.

"Here's an example. Jesus' teaching 'Love thy neighbor as thyself' has remained alive for centuries. In part, the importance of the Old Testament idea kept it alive. It also survived because Jesus gave it a powerful ThoughtForm, and other people, the disciples, assimilated it, gave it impetus and sent it further. The commandment has now endured for centuries."

I didn't disagree with the possibility that Karen's Thought-Forms worked, but I had to ask the obvious English-teacher question. "Didn't this thought survive because it was written into a language and transmitted?"

"Of course that's true, but wouldn't you concede that many ideas are written and scarcely survive past a few hours? The fact that this was *born* as consciousness of great potential and was sent with tremendous impetus insured its survival."

Karen added another idea. "If ThoughtForms are created but sent to no particular person, they eventually enter a general sphere of activity or movement or influence. They tend to collect in groups. Just as certain varieties of plants, grow in a particular area or people find communal living an advantage, so Thought-Forms do also. Such grouping can create more powerful Thought-Forms.

"ThoughtForms collect in pools and support each other in two ways. In some instances they finally move out with greater impact into the society of human consciousness. The two types—human consciousness and thought consciousness—blend, further support each other, and evolve.

"In other instances, ThoughtForms seemingly die. However, nothing really dies but simply recycles. When a living organism dies, its body returns to earth to nourish other life forms. When thoughts seemingly die, they collect in pools and give power to other ThoughtForms. While the individual ThoughtForm may die, its substance remains and nourishes others.

"By the way, Mom," Karen digressed temporarily, "you have wondered how this writing works. I do exactly what I am describing. I create abstract ThoughtForms. These are powerful enough that you can receive them without hearing my voice; you simply receive them on your mental screen. The actual writing only clarifies and aids retention. Without the writing, you would almost immediately forget what you received. And because you are word-oriented, you translate ideas into words."

The writing seemed to anticipate my question. "Yes, we use word-language here," the pen continued, "but we use more than word-language, too. ThoughtForms are universal language more powerful than words. You already have a hint of this on your plane. Nonverbal symbols—pictures, music—can make more direct impact on your consciousness than can words.

"But more than this can take place on my plane and between you and me. I use neither words nor nonverbal symbols. I impress ThoughtForms directly on your mind. You receive them and translate them into words. You select the words you think appropriate. Most of the time, the way you structure a sentence doesn't matter. The idea matters.

"In the beginning of the writing you experienced double consciousness because your receptive screen had to be open to receive the ThoughtForm. At the same time, your mind had to take over and translate. So you felt as if you operated on two levels of consciousness at once."

I said, "But sometimes you struggle to get a particular word in the writing."

"Only when I want to be absolutely accurate with definitions."

My only contact with such concepts as universal language was in literature, with an author like Yeats. I said, "Suppose I don't know the universal language or symbols you use, then how do I translate them into words and ideas?"

"I use ThoughtForms mainly from your own experience," came Karen's reply. "You are widely read and educated. From this you have acquired many ThoughtForms. You may be little aware of them consciously, but as long as you have contacted them, I can use them. I have been taught to recognize which ThoughtForms are a part of your experience, and I use those.

"Also, when ThoughtForms collect in pools, people often absorb them from the pools into individual consciousness. Through such direct absorption, you know many universal ThoughtForms. I can use these."

I interrupted. "You haven't told me the technique of borning ThoughtForms yet, but I have one more question. Don't those who practice prayer techniques, such as the followers of Unity and Christian Science, already use your methods?"

"Of course those who use prayer techniques are using powerful thought. However, their methods are often inadequate or the practitioners inept.

"Such people tend to use only visual imagery. For example, a healer may project a mental picture of an afflicted person as being well. The more vivid the picture, the more likely healing will take place. In this case the healer projects a *kind* of ThoughtForm. Visual imagery alone is only partially effective. ThoughtForms use all of the senses and more. Abstract thought can acquire an actual shape. This involves a three-part process: creating, waiting, and sending."

"Are we finally to the 'how to'"? I asked.

"For a teacher who insists on giving students detail, you're certainly impatient." The pen squiggled, then paused dramatically.

"Step one involves placing the ThoughtForm in space. This requires *sensualization*, an extension of visualization. In the latter, you create a vivid *image* of an object, person, or situation. When you sensualize, you create the same image using *all* of its sensory properties. This may require considerable effort on your part. The more vividly you can learn to sensualize, the more powerful your potential ThoughtForm. If you are trying to create a ThoughtForm for an abstract idea, you should use known symbols.

"Let's try a simple example. Suppose you wish to create a ThoughtForm of love for another person. Traditionally the heart shape represents love. Begin to add to that image. You might next choose an appropriate color. If the recipient is a sexual partner, you would probably choose red. For a friend or relative you might select rose. To express sympathy, a gold heart would be appropriate, and for spiritual love, blue or lavender."

Karen directed me to a book describing aura and the meanings of colors in aura. As usual, she wrote about these colors before I read the book, and they proved to be accurate for the standard colors recognized by psychics as those representing these particular emotions. She said, "Make the color as luminous as possible for visualizing the heart."

She continued, "Next, work with your other senses. Include a scent, perhaps floral, that represents the type of love you wish to express. Remember that the rose is not the only flower that represents love. The pungency of geranium or the sweetness of honeysuckle might be appropriate for a particular person. For touch, try the texture of satin, fur, skin. In addition to the obvious taste of candy, consider pomegranate or orange. Use the sound of the flute as well as the violin. Spend as much time and energy as is necessary for selecting the appropriate elements of the sensualization."

I had a question I wanted Karen to answer. "When you described kicking Jim on the shin, you said you were surprised that he felt it physically. Were you using a ThoughtForm? What did you include to give it power?"

She squiggled. "I'm almost embarrassed to tell you. It was really primitive, but remember I had only been here a few days. Here it comes. My message was, 'Stay in school. You and I worked too hard for you to give up now. Are you a man or aren't you? To get that message accross, here's what I used.

Touch: gum on his shoe (Jim hated that) to tell him to stick to his goal.

Taste: Heineken beer to remind him to be a man.

Smell: pipe tobacco also to remind him to be a man.

Sight: diploma, cap, and gown to show him the goal.

Hearing: my voice yelling at him.

"See how easy it can be? At the last minute, I asked Sarah for help, and she asked the right question: 'How do you plan to get his attention?'

" 'Kick him,' I said almost without thinking.

" 'Do it,' She said.

"Even that ThoughtForm wouldn't have worked if I had kept my frustration in check. But I'm getting ahead of myself. That's for the third stage."

"I'm glad you don't get that frustrated with me. Or do you?"

"I'm more likely to give you a bad grade," she teased.

She got us back to business. "Second, place the ThoughtForm in 'time.' Any life that gets born must be incubated—given time to form and develop. When I used to write my essays for school, I wrote several drafts. Then I set the last one aside for a few days. When I came back to it, I knew where it needed revision, and I knew when it was ready for someone else to read. This works the same way.

"Place your sensualization in a warm, dark place to hatch. This means you should try to ignore it, put it out of your mind. *No anxious peeking to see if it is ready.*"

"How long do I wait?" I asked. "Minutes? Hours? Days?"

"That depends on the situation. Trust your own instinct. You'll know when the time is right."

I hoped so.

Like a school teacher outlining a lesson, Karen said, "Third, combine 'time' and 'space' by putting the ThoughtForm in motion. To do this, you must share with it your own frequency. Work with the sensualization until you can internalize it—until it becomes a part of your very being and you can at any given moment bring all its elements to mind readily.

"It's not just a matter of knowing the ThoughtForm thoroughly but of merging with it. To bring it to life, you must literally give it some of your life-essence or frequency. Be sure you merge, become one, with your sensualization to give it full life potential.

"Now put the ThoughtForm in motion. Human emotion comes

close to experiencing frequency. Select an emotion suitable to the ThoughtForm being generated, but more important, send it with strong impetus.

"For the most part, avoid negative emotion such as anger. With the ThoughtForm I created to contact Jim, I kicked. However, I kicked not out of anger but from frustration and caring. I'm sure the tremendous emotional impetus I gave to the one for Jim was the reason he actually felt the kick."

I tried making ThoughtForms. It was slow going. Karen was accurate when she said that finding symbols appropriate to the idea was easy. I had fun trying to make them fit the thought I wanted to convey.

I found the second step more difficult than it sounded. My tendency to analyze stood in the way. I constantly questioned whether I would have done better with this image or that odor.

The third step baffled me. Engendering an emotion is not all that easy for me. It seemed too artificial trying to "pump up" joy or excitement. Finally Karen helped.

"You can gain power," she said, "by acquiring it from other forms of consciousness. What you are after is life-essence. During stage one, in addition to sensualizing, actually use plants, animals, or even other humans and pull their frequency to you. The frequency of consciousness is available in other forms of life.

"You usually acquire it, literally. by eating life-essence. More appropriately, you can acquire it by absorption. Sit near a plant or animal. Talk to it and ask it to share with you its essence, offering, of course, to share yours with it. Then sit quietly. Contemplate that plant or animal and endeavor to share essence. It will happen with no more effort than that. As you absorb such force, you will find it transformed into usable frequency.

"Some people are more cerebral than emotional, and your ThoughtForm can also gain its impetus through spoken words. If emotion doesn't work for you, then give birth to your Thought-Form with the impetus of a spoken 'Let there be . . .'"

This last suggestion worked better for me. I couldn't rationally explain what happened, but my life was less troubled and far happier because of this sharing of life essences with other forms of consciousness.

"By the way, Mom," Karen said, thinking, I suppose, that I might get too proud of my efforts, "don't worry about your ThoughtForms being too powerful or dangerous. Most of the ThoughtForms from your world weigh in as wimps—the content trivial, the projection negligible. They die in infancy."

"Have a good vacation," Karen said when I finished this portion of the writing.

Tom and I were off to Arizona to visit my childhood home town, Jerome. "What will you be doing?" I asked Karen.

"Traveling. But our travel is different. Getting from 'here' to 'there' poses no problem for us because we have no here or there. Think about that when you're taking planes and driving."

I did, often, during the next two weeks.

Karen's last words were, "Don't run into any obstructed thought."

14

CHAPTER

"IN YOUR WORLD you bump up against so many obstructed thoughts, you should all carry thought insurance."

"Obstructed in what way?" I asked.

Karen answered, "Partial truths and thoughts that go beyond their logical conclusions. Partial truths can become greater obstructions than totally negative thoughts. Negative thoughts are easily recognized and destroyed. Partial truths tend to live on unnoticed."

"Can you give an example?" I asked.

"Hundreds. In the obstructed universe, glimpses of truths become 'fact.' These glimpses can warp a society because they are believed as fact and operated upon as truth. The Domino Theory, for example, is such a thought that extended into the Vietnam war and threatened to destroy several societies.

"Obstructed thought happens because of the tendency of the human brain to pigeonhole and classify, which can lead to rigid thinking. The classification process gives birth to inflexible or incomplete ThoughtForms. This happens in medicine, for example, where the scientific method should be the most flexible and open to new ideas.

"Medicine can only come out of the witch-doctor phase of knives and potions when it learns to recognize the reality of a spiritual body, aura, essences, and ThoughtForms. Medicine has taken half-truths and extended them without considering alternative cures."

That statement got my attention. We had certainly relied on doctors with Karen's illness, and those doctors had used knives and potions. Was she trying to tell me we shouldn't have?

"I'm not saying doctors are no good," the writing continued as though reading my thoughts. "I am saying that you should learn other methods of healing that can aid doctors and eventually replace current medical techniques. Relate this to our own family's attempts at prayer. However, the kind of healing I want to show you, posits certain assumptions that your medical science doesn't accept."

Karen quickly drew a simple human stick figure. Then she drew a recognizable human form around it. From the second body, she extended rays outward in all directions.

"Here's the reality," she said. "The stick man is a person in your world. The full figure with the rays of light is a person in my world. What you fail to realize is that you live in both of these bodies now. Your physical body is encased in your spiritual body, They coexist.

"Mom, you can see aura around people—the colored light that surrounds bodies."

I had first noticed the colored light surrounding people when I was a child. I thought everyone saw it. One day I mentioned it to my minister father, and he hit me for talking about it. I quickly learned not only to stay quiet about what I saw, but also to quit seeing it.

In adulthood, during the time I learned and practiced meditation techniques, I again began to see auras. I prefer not to, so I normally shut them out. But when it happens, it's usually because I am in the presence of someone I can help.

It happened one day as I approached Tom on the street. As he walked toward me, I saw his aura. His usual blue and yellow colors seemed murky, and a hole appeared in the upper right quadrant of his abdomen.

"You don't feel well," I said.

"Gas pains, I guess."

"See a doctor," I urged. I explained what I had seen. "Something's wrong."

A month later Tom had his gall bladder removed.

❀ ❀ ❀

In the writing, Karen said, "The aura is the key to genuine and permanent healing. Psychics who see aura can tell when the aura is distorted or disturbed. As you did with Dad, they can see disease.

"If the aura can be a diagnostic tool, then it can also be a healing tool. Logically, if the aura can be repaired, the physical body will be repaired as well. Yet modern medicine doesn't even begin to recognize this possibility. Instead, doctors follow ancient and more primitive methods of diagnosis and treatment.

"In early times, people observed that an external injury to the body could be healed by cutting. Later, doctors used surgery to remove or repair internal injuries also. It was a glimpse of truth. They perfected and refined surgical methods so that we no longer imagine any other way to heal an ailing gall bladder or heart.

"Through trial and error, primitive man discovered that when his stomach hurt, he could ingest certain plants and stop the ache. Now you ingest pills, substitutes for the plants. Sometimes the pills do harm, so you test them, classify and categorize bits of information to make sure you don't hurt too many people. You have even set up a governmental agency to protect citizens from injurious medicines."

I expressed my own belief about another area of medicine. I said, "Freud convinced us that experiences buried in the unconscious mind can cause emotional stress and physical illness. Hasn't this glimpse of a significant truth also become an obstructed thought?"

Karen, who had once planned to become a psychologist, agreed. She told me, "The idea of the unconscious as a source of illness has become an easy way out for the doctor who lacks knowledge about a physical problem. If he can't find the cause of the pain, he can blame it on a psychological problem.

"All the methods we've discussed work. But because of partial truths that have led to obstructions in thought, we ignore other possible sources of curing disease. Partial truths have become major obstructions."

I asked, "How is aura a possible way of performing healing in our world?"

"Let me describe how we see aura. Mom, when you are healthy, I 'see' your spiritual body as having beautiful color, light, sound, texture, and fragrance. By the particular arrangement of these attributes I recognize you. Illness in your spiritual body affects your physical body. When the spiritual body's color is dull, the texture rough, I know your physical body will become damaged or diseased."

Karen emphasized her point. *"Injury to the spiritual body causes disease in the physical body."*

"How does the spiritual body become injured?" I asked.

"In your world, your spiritual body is vulnerable through its aura. In your obstructed environment, you contact many non-human forms of consciousness. You recognize the biological forms. Others—forms of energy such as electric, atomic, solar—escape you as being forms of consciousness at all. Nevertheless, they are, and they also have auras. Their auras constantly merge with yours.

"Both positive and negative effects on your physical and spiritual bodies happen in two ways: the sharing of essence of life-force or frequency with other forms of consciousness, and the use of ThoughtForms."

The pen stopped abruptly. When it began again a minute later, Karen wrote, "It's time to practice what we preach. I see your aura dimming. We want you well, so let's finish another day. Meanwhile, lie down and our medics will replenish your aura."

I slept, and an hour later awoke refreshed and energetic.

Three days later, Karen wrote, "The ultimate purpose of the universe is the development—the evolution—of higher and higher spiritual consciousness. For evolution to take place, many forms of consciousness must interact. But evolution functions best when the interaction is selective rather than random. When two forms of consciousness merge, they automatically share their essences through their frequencies. Some forms blend easily while others, more alien to one another, can cause harm unless they merge carefully.

"Here's an example from your world where essences merge literally and physically. You eat a piece of meat. The meat actually becomes a part of your own physical body. But to accomplish this, you have destroyed the animal's physical life. Since nothing really dies, the animal is now in my world. If it was the proper time for the animal to die because it had filled its potential on earth and no longer needs its physical body, then sharing essence with you in this manner brings you no harm. However, if the animal should not have died, then its essence can harm yours.

"Obviously you can't always know what state prevails. So-called primitive people follow a custom of talking to the plant or animal they have killed. They apologize for taking away the physical life of one form of consciousness to sustain another. Your own custom of prayer before meals probably has its origins in such intuitive knowledge.

"What I have said about eating other forms of consciousness is true at a psychological level as well. Think of the fact that so many people have pets. This custom recognizes the spiritual fact of different forms of consciousness sharing essences. Do it consciously, and you will probably eat less meat, but don't necessarily give up meat entirely. Let your body guide you."

I liked that idea. "I assume it's all right to eat plants."

"As long as you live in your world, your physical body needs nourishment. Become aware of your physical appetites. When you crave certain foods, eat them. Also actively look for ways to share essences harmlessly. Sit under a tree, smell a flower, listen to a waterfall. Share essences with other forms of consciousness as harmlessly as possible. As you do this, you will become less interested in eating certain foods such as beef and pork."

117

I wanted to know about sharing human essence. "I know we can be damaged by negative people, but what about the leeches who absorb my frequency without giving any back?"

"They drain you," Karen said. "They intend no harm, but they are spongers who pilfer your frequency and soak up your aura. Being with them makes you tired, even ill.

"You can protect yourself from the drainers. Barricade your aura when drainers like these are around. Use sensualization with images, odors, and sounds to shut them out so they can't filch from your aura."

I asked, "Of all the possible ways of improving individual consciousness through sharing frequency, how do we decide what to choose?"

"Choose according to purpose. Plant, animal, and human give needed biological essence. Atomic, solar, electrical, and other such forms of consciousness offer cosmic frequencies, powerful but alien. Be cautious in your use of these.

"Use ThoughtForms. They are the most efficacious, forceful, compatible."

In the days ahead she would elaborate more on ThoughtForms and their use.

15
CHAPTER

"Why are we born?"

"I'll defer to you on that one," I told Karen.

"Let me give you the parallel question," she said. "Why do we die?"

"It's still your turn."

"The answer to both questions: *To serve evolution—the purpose of the universe.*"

"You've said that before."

"I have indeed." The tone of Karen's pen was amused and sardonic. "It's crucial that you grasp this, so you will comprehend my further discussion of obstructed thought.

"Here's something else I've said before. *Consciousness is the only reality. All degrees of consciousness are in evolution.*

"Such evolution is not alone physical as your world sees it but is also mental and spiritual. Humans with their ability to think, have progressed through considerable mental evolution on your side as well as on mine. So far most spiritual evolution is taking place on my side. This is because evolution on your plane is *quantitative.* Evolution on my plane is *qualitative.* Let me explain.

"Each individual consciousness is born on earth plane with a certain degree or level or *quality* of consciousness. It's like saying a person is born with a certain innate level of spiritual capacity and a certain unique spiritual 'personality' with set boundaries, not only as a human being, but as a particular human being.

"This spiritual degree or level or quality cannot be altered while your individual consciousness remains in your obstructed world. When individual consciousness passes to my side, it is free to develop additional quality.

"Quality can evolve in my world; it is fixed in yours."

119

That perturbed me. I had to ask, "If we haven't the capability of modifying our quality in our world, then why are we born here at all?"

"Because in your world you develop quantity.

"Each individual consciousness is also born with a certain *quantity* of consciousness. Your job there is to enlarge and develop your unique spiritual personality by acquiring quantity, more of what you already are. You make your quality (your innate spiritual personality) richer through the goals and experiences you choose for yourself there."

Karen said, "To sum up, we are free to develop quantity in both the obstructed and unobstructed universe. We evolve quality in the unobstructed universe."

She waited for me to absorb that. "How do I develop quantity?"

"Let me amplify the picture. While the central purpose of the universe is evolution (also called progress), each individual consciousness serves one or more of six other purposes: Light, Truth, Healing, Building, Production, and Justice. These are called the Seven Purposes. Whichever one you serve indicates your quality, your destiny in your world. Your job in your world is to serve your purpose as fully as possible."

"How do I know which purpose I am destined to serve?"

"It's innate. You are born with a particular purpose to serve. You recognize your purpose through a natural inclination. Think about why you're a teacher. Your love of learning automatically chose you to serve Truth and Light. Your individual purpose *chooses* you. The purpose you serve in your world matches your quality."

"Wait a minute," I protested. "My purpose *chooses* me? I don't buy all this destiny stuff. What ever happened to free will?"

She chuckled with the pen. "It's there too. You may choose any particular path you like to serve your purpose. To serve the purpose of Truth, you could have been a researcher, a writer, or taken any other job that fulfills that purpose. You could also have defied your purpose and chosen to serve Building."

"And would my defiance, my defection to the purpose of Building, have caused me to smack my thumb every time I pounded a nail?"

"Nothing so blatant. But you would probably have felt dissatisfied and unfulfilled in your work. People unhappy in their jobs are often serving a purpose they are not suited for. In fact, some people may not recognize their purposes clearly. Some may fail to serve any purpose at all. Others may serve for the wrong reasons. Consider, for example, the doctor interested in medicine as a high calling versus the one who only wants fame or money. The first collects much quantity; the second collects far less. The more quantity you acquire there, the easier your transition here.

"Do your job."

She had more to say, "When you enter my world, the quantity you have gained in yours enters a universal pool of consciousness and increases all quality of consciousness. Thus, while you are fulfilling your destiny, you are also adding to the universal quality. This is important, for from this pool quality is reborn into specific entities of consciousness back on your plane. In this way you make your contribution to the great purpose—progress or evolution.

"Do your job.

"While evolution takes place at all levels inevitably, note that when consciousness reaches a stage of mental evolution, as in man, it begins to participate actively in the evolutionary process. By consciously adding to your quantity in your world, you advance evolution. And when you come to my world having acquired much individual quantity, you will have earned the right to begin to serve other purposes and gain quality. In the unobstructed world we are 'destined' to increase our quality.

"Do your job."

Karen had more to say about gaining quantity and how it benefits us personally.

"Any quantity you can add to yourself in your world reveals

itself in your aura. The intensified aura can protect and heal your physical body. More important, when you come here, it will surround and house your spiritual body.

"I have suggested ThoughtForms as one way to improve aura. You can also ask us for help.

"Many people here can help you directly with your growth. We do it with ThoughtForms and by sharing our essences with you. You only need to ask. Then open yourself. Be receptive and porous."

"Is that last word right?" I asked.

"Your spiritual body, the real you," the answer came, "is made of much finer substance than your physical body. The old ghost movies showing the wraithlike figure were a glimpse. Your spiritual body is porous."

"And whom do I ask?" I wanted to know. "Do I 'pray' to Karen for assistance in my petty problems? Surely you have better things to do."

"You bet I do, but I'll try to spare you a few minutes." Karen's caustic wit was typical of her.

She became serious. "One of the most important jobs one can have over here is that of guide. Guides can act directly in your world. One of the great glimpses of earlier times was that of the guardian angel, for that is what a guide is.

"Not everyone in your world has a personal guide and certainly not everyone here has this as a job. Although the guide can help you with problems—she or he can give such assistance when you ask—but a strict law of the universe constrains us. *No one may interfere in another's opportunity to learn and progress.*

"Remember what I have just said, so you and I don't allow a glimpse to become another obstructed thought. The guide's job is to aid an individual's spiritual growth and progress, the goal of evolution."

I wanted to know, "How do guides work?"

"Guides are not assigned. Saint Peter doesn't call me in and tell me to go help you. You attract a guide whose quality of consciousness matches yours. In addition, you attract a guide according to how much effort you put into gaining quantity. You earn spiritual guidance. Thus, even those of lower degree on your side can acquire guides by their own efforts at spiritual growth."

"That helps," I said. "After hearing that, I don't resent the predestination idea quite so much."

"I knew you'd come around. But here's a warning. Don't try to attract a guide unless you're sure you want one. As with every other relationship, there are obligations. For you, attracting a guide means you must become an active participant in your own growth. Your efforts must match those of the guide. Otherwise the spiritual pull from the guide can overpower you.

"This is *one* explanation of suffering. Because you fail to fulfill your part in your own spiritual development, a gap develops between your activities and those of your guide. Such a gap can result in pain for you, a sort of spiritual growth pang.

"On the positive side, such pain and growth struggle is never wasted if one learns from it. Your very attitude toward the suffering provides growth. And from this side your pains, your sufferings, appear trivial, for we see them as a part of the total process of evolution. Our perspective broadens, and time and space diminish in importance. Pain teaches much if you are spiritually porous."

I didn't much like the 'God rewards pain' idea. I said, "It sounds like I should be happy to suffer so I can grow."

"Not at all," Karen assured me. "No one needs to suffer. Suffering comes when you 'bump up' against a universal law. Here's another encompassing insight. You 'suffer' when you break a law of the unobstructed universe. The fact that you don't recognize the law doesn't matter. It functions regardless of your cognizance of it.

"Here's an example. Despite the fact that you have no family history of heart disease, that you watch your diet, that you exercise, that you avoid stress, you have a heart attack. 'Undeserved,' you shout. 'I observed all the laws of the obstructed world. It isn't fair.'

"But you did break a law of the unobstructed world. Your difficulty was in your failure to protect your spiritual body. By developing quantity and earning a guide, you could have circumvented your suffering. A guide might not have kept you from dying. Everything dies. But you could have accomplished your dying, your transition, more easily. A guide could have helped you die in your sleep.

"Universal law does give us free will, Mom. We can *choose* to evolve or not. Parallel laws exist in both worlds. We can choose to develop quantity there and quality here. When we choose to evolve, we avoid the 'bump' called suffering."

She gave an encouraging thought. "Parents can acquire a guide for a child by their efforts. Suppose you wonder if your child is of the high quality that automatically attracts a guide. The parents, or those interested in the child's welfare, can call a guide to that ward by their desire.

"This was once the purpose of infant baptism, a glimpse of spiritual truth that has often been distorted into magic and superstition. The religious ceremony that included the cleansing of the soul with specially blessed water and the laying on of hands could be used to attract a spirit guide. One who acquires a guide in infancy can avoid the problems of the spiritual gaps mentioned before."

She gave more good news. "Once you attract a personal guide, you will always keep one. A new guide may be called as you acquire quantity. Once you attract a very spiritual guide, that one remains with you until you no longer need one. The guide may remain with you even without your need and after you come here."

I asked, "What about those who don't acquire a personal guide?"

"They are helped through group or team methods. A team on our side serves a group of people on your side. Such people on your side need not be linked by family ties or geography. The connection is determined by purpose.

"Groups that have common goals work best. The goal could even be seemingly detrimental, such as fighting a war, for this unites them in a common cause. Purpose counts most in grouping for guide work; goals only provide a handhold or temporary way in, but communal instinct among you works to the advantage of guides here."

I was still disturbed that so much of one's life seemed predetermined by quality of consciousness and purpose. I saw this as discouraging. The writing halted for about a week, apparently to avoid coloring or bias from my mind. When it resumed, it went like this:

"There should be no discouragement because one is born with particular attributes. You have always known this was so. Look at the reflection of this on your plane. For example, look at those born with mental or physical handicaps. Such people can overcome these handicaps by attitude and effort. Such handicaps may or may not be a detriment when it comes to developing quantity. The handicapped person may indeed have an advantage.

"Your perspective of time causes much of your dismay. Time doesn't exist as you know it. The unobstructed universe has no 'span' of 'time.' Acquiring quantity 'before' 'beginning' to work on quality does not 'slow' you down.

"Those who have practiced reincarnation have made too much of the idea of destiny. Let's look at that next."

After she dropped the pen, I realized she hadn't really answered her original questions about why we are born and die. I would challenge her with that.

16
CHAPTER

"HERE WE GO for another 'bump' up against obstructed thought.

"Those who have practiced reincarnation have insisted that one has a destiny and that it is necessary to work out one's karma on earth plane before one can go on to other planes of experience.

"Here again is one of those obstructed thoughts. We do have a kind of destiny and a kind of karma–serving our purpose and developing quantity. However, because we cannot develop more quality and serve additional purposes on earth, we limit ourselves by trying to come back and 'do it over.'

"Whatever amount of quantity we develop in one lifetime is sufficient. Repetition of earth experience isn't necessary for further development of quantity, for little is added in a second trial.

"And even more, such a belief shows a limitation of understanding of what happens in my world. Our job here is the development of greater quality. The individual who fails to take the opportunity to develop quality here because he wants to reincarnate there, not only fails himself but the purpose of evolution as well.

"The reincarnationists, those who believe in literal rebirth of an individual consciousness in the obstructed world, have obstructed the idea of quality and quantity. They have taken a partial truth and made it a hard-binding and destructive dogma."

She repeated some of what she had said before, presumably to be sure it related to the obstructed idea of reincarnation. "Destiny relates mainly to your plane: the destiny of purpose and quality. Freedom of choice to evolve happens in our unobstructed world. Here our freedom is unlimited. So why would anyone want to return to a limited part of life's adventure in the obstructed when free and limitless opportunities lie ahead? Here you can develop freely all aspects of your consciousness. Here, you can serve the great purpose of evolution. Here, you truly work out your karma.

"The reincarnationist answers, 'If I develop enough quantity in one lifetime, I can come back with a higher quality the next time.' But the universal law insists that evolution of quality takes place in the unobstructed world."

I asked, "Why is this so important? What harm does it do?"

"The idea of reincarnation is a great glimpse. There is such a thing as reincarnation of *quality* of consciousness. Various degrees of quality of consciousness are constantly being reborn, but they should not be reborn as individual entities coming back. Individual consciousness does not die and should not be reborn in the obstructed. It should continue on my plane and on other planes beyond mine."

I wanted to know, "What happens when individuals come across?"

"Glad you asked," said Karen. "They bring with them quantity from their earth living. The individual keeps his personal quantity and a like amount goes into a general reservoir of quality of consciousness on this side. Earth parents, through their own spiritual quality and quantity, are then able to draw from the reservoir and pass on a specific quality to a newborn child.

"The child gradually acquires quantity and adds it to the reservoir of consciousness when she comes across. She leavens the spiritual level of the whole, much or little, depending on what she adds. Those who add little often wish they had lived more fully. This, in fact, is the equivalent of the final judgment. The judgment is one of self-condemnation for the lack of quantity contributed.

"And this is where the reincarnationist stumbles in. She judges herself, determines that she should have gained more quantity, and decides to try it again. Sadly, a second incarnation in the obstructed universe (and it does happen) scarcely adds to the pool of consciousness at all. The main purpose of consciousness–

evolution—is not really advanced by literal reincarnation. The person who continues here and develops quality serves evolution better."

I was intrigued with the consistency of logic in Karen's description. But what about the many problems reincarnation theory seemed to solve? Certainly other mediums more talented than myself had promoted this theory. It did seem to answer the question of suffering, though it was beginning to look as if Karen's theory did too, and perhaps more intelligently. What about the often recognized feeling of *déja vu*, the feeling of having been there or experienced something before, that reincarnationists claim is explained by their theory. I let the pen run on at its own pace to see what came.

"Actually," said the writing, "reincarnation explains less than the idea of direct immortality. You note, Mom, that other psychics believed in reincarnation, but many do not. Often psychics of the reincarnation persuasion are accurate in making other predictions. They base much of their ability to predict or heal on the fact that they see past lives. Therefore, they claim to know why the person is now ill or behaving in a certain manner. However, they don't offer *proof* that the person actually did live such a life. They only claim it.

"Mediums who believe in direct immortality also heal, predict the future, and explain events by saying someone in the next world told them. And here, often more proof is more convincing. It is more impressive for Karen, or anyone here, to produce specific evidence of her own life that can be validated than to claim with no proof that she lived before.

"Mom, all any psychic can do is offer information for its inherent value and let others decide what to accept. I believe what I am telling you will be so logical that many will accept it."

I raised the same question I had earlier in this session. "What specific harm does this theory do?"

Karen answered directly this time. "Confusion creates serious difficulties for both worlds. When we come across, we are the same selves we've always been. We retain our personalities and prejudices. Those who come across believing in reincarnation still believe it over here. They attempt to reenter a body there and be reborn. This creates situations that the rest of us view with dismay.

"Your world is intended as a borning place where all life is new. Everyone is intended to be a first-time individual. If the reincarnationist is spiritually stronger than the new consciousness being born (and sometimes this is true, for they tend to select lower qualities to invade), he supplants that new consciousness. The new being, then, is not able to develop; on arrival here at death the being is only a partially developed consciousness. The two parts of the being usually separate here, and of course, this creates considerable confusion. Both need much help. And sadly, the reincarnationist may still be unconvinced and try again to be reborn.

"In other cases a person may choose to be reborn in a new consciousness of a higher quality. Then the newborn dominates and develops but still is considerably damaged by the interference. The reincarnated person is submerged and for a time becomes a lost soul. From this you can see our aversion to the concept of literal reincarnation.

"Reincarnation plays havoc with the development of quantity. And, by the way, we do not call this process reincarnation. We call it possession."

I was bothered. "If what you say is true, why do people try to reincarnate?"

"Those who firmly believe are difficult to convince. Such people believe they will be handicapped if they are not reborn. They assume that the only way to develop karma is to re-experience earth life.

"Also, many people are *embedded* in the physical. To us some of you look like those little plastic souvenir paperweights with tiny fish or plant life embedded in them; you are bits of frozen consciousness implanted in the material world. Once you postulate and accept that the unobstructed universe exists, once you believe that life is potentially more beautiful than anything on earth, you would think people would prefer it. Yet for many, the physical world is the real world. It's all they have, and they cling covetously to it. Poor souls!

"A psychological reason is more disturbing and difficult to combat. Some people reincarnate as a form of self-punishment because of guilt. The impact of coming across is devastating, for often they see vividly the mistakes they made. They experience a period of deep regret. Some desire so strongly to try again and do a better job (work out their karma) that they are difficult to convince that they will only compound their problems through such an effort.

"Worse, their guilt over past mistakes makes them want to punish themselves by repeating a miserable experience. 'If I can suffer this time for what I did before,' they say, 'then I can atone for the past.' We try to convince them that any atonement can be accomplished here, but this is futile if the guilt is very deep."

I wanted to know about individuals that claimed to be associated with the same people again and again over many lifetimes. "Why would they want this?"

Karen's answer showed a depressing aspect of human nature. "Attempted reincarnation is sometimes the result of a deep hostility toward others. Suppose that you and I were mother and daughter in the most recent life but might have been sisters in a previous life and a married couple at another time. They claim they can better correct the mistakes made with the same people. Could it not also be that they unconsciously desire to further punish another person for past injuries as well? A hostile individual would secretly desire this."

I asked another question. "Many claim that the common experience of *déja vu* is evidence of reincarnation. They say that the sense of having experienced a time or place before is simply the recognition of a previous life. Are they right?"

"Partially. You remember I told you that quantity of consciousness goes into a reservoir and is reborn. Although this is converted into quality, the *memory* of the quantity is left in the reservoir. This memory of life-experience can be reborn into a new consciousness, a new individual.

"This easily explains *déja vu*. Suppose a new individual acquires some of my quantity memory, perhaps the experience of being in the hospital in Los Angeles. At some point in his life, if he himself enters that hospital or one that looks like it, he will doubtless experience not only a strong feeling of having been there before but also some negative emotions connected with it.

"The fact that such experiences are fairly common among many people but are not consistently frequent in a given individual is more readily explained by the reincarnation of memory from the pool than by literal individual reincarnation.

"Have you ever considered the very curious circumstance that no one while on earth really remembers a past experience of life. Do you? Did I? A few *think* they do. And granted, a very few parapsychologists cite cases of reincarnation in which very young children appear to remember past lives. These could just as well be cases of possession. They could also be cases of mediumship in which the child is telling the story of someone actually on my side but making it appear as if he is telling his own story. Thus no real proof of 'remembering' is given.

"Some say the memory of the past remains unconscious, but this is a cop-out. It would seem that if one is to correct past mistakes, work out his karma, he could do a better job of it if he remembered what went wrong before. Indeed, anything less would appear to be a kind of strange punishment of a most unethical universe.

"Endless repetition of experience that teaches nothing because nothing experienced is remembered, is the worst possible hell–a form of cruel and unusual punishment by a merciless God. At the very least, there is certainly an oddity in the confusion of going back to earth for fifty trips and learning so little."

I tuned in to Karen's last statements. The logic made sense. Karen's comments about the cruelty of trying to atone for past mistakes when one does not even remember them was a telling point. But I was still concerned about the concept of suffering, for I had always felt reincarnation was a logical explanation for seemingly inexplicable illness or poverty.

She was ready. "Can't you see how this is an oversimplified explanation for suffering?" she asked. "The reincarnationists have used their karma theory as a handy-dandy tool for explaining a very complex problem. The supreme level of consciousness is positive. No vindictive God metes out punishment with no opportunity to make amends nor any memory of past experience."

"But," I said, "your explanation that we bump up against laws we don't know about is equally disturbing. Why should I suffer for not knowing a law?"

"Because the universal law is put there for a larger purpose than causing or understanding suffering. It is in place to provide order and continuity for the entire universe. We live in a universe of a complex system of moral and spiritual laws as well as physical ones. Inevitably, because of our limited earth-bound knowledge, we are going to make mistakes that will result in what we call suffering. However, knowledge of the law is accessible to us if we wish to investigate."

That made sense.

I realized that Karen had effectively answered her own questions about why we are born and why we die. We are born as individual consciousnesses so that we can ultimately further the purpose of the evolution of all consciousness. We die for the same reason. Taking care to be born in the obstructed world only once gives an individual consciousness the greatest opportunity to serve the evolutionary purpose.

17

CHAPTER

"DEATH with dignity."

"Suicide is a sin."

"Right to life."

"Such a fuss you people make about death. In chapter fifteen I asked, 'Why are we born?' and answered 'To serve the purpose of evolution of consciousness.'

"I also asked, 'Why do we die?'

"The answer is, 'We don't. Individual consciousness lives on.'

"That fact puts a new perspective on some of your concerns about 'how' we make the transition to the unobstructed world."

"Do you mean suicide?" I asked.

"Suicide, euthanasia. Much of what I tell you will be controversial but only because thought has been obstructed for so long in western culture."

"I suppose you're right," I conceded. "If death is but a step into a new level of consciousness where the individual continues to grow, then the problem of mercy killing is of considerably less significance than we have made it."

"Caution," Karen said. "I want to make absolutely clear the level of mercy makes euthansia acceptable. In our world, we believe it should take place in cases of definite terminal illness—if the individual is a vegetable or if his suffering is so intense that prolongation of life even with drugs is abhorrent. In such cases someone must take responsibility for the *release into life,* into our world. I do not mean merely removing life-support systems and letting the person go on but sending him on by literally destroying the physical body.

"In instances where the mental capacity is so limited that no further learning from life experience can take place, the person deserves release into *unobstructed* life. I grant that the imminence of death is easier to judge than determining how extreme the mental impairment must be. In general, a person who needs total care of essential bodily functions deserves release.

"Beyond these cases there are those who should be sent across, such as the individual of minimal IQ who can acquire little or no quantity. The test is this: *If quantity can no longer be gained on earth plane due to extreme physical handicaps, then coming across is necessary for growth.* Such a termination truly releases the individual.

"Of course your laws would have to be changed so that the person who performs the release is not punished. Obviously, strict controls would be needed to determine what is mercy and what is indulgence. Obviously too, there will doubtless be abuses of such laws, especially at first. But we believe this can and will be controlled. And we see this as an enlightened view of the obstructed thought, 'Thou shalt not kill (ever).'"

"How should this be done?" I asked. "Most doctors don't want to, and certainly loved ones find it difficult."

"Until you learn better methods, such so-called mercy killing should be accomplished by physical (medically induced) means. More doctors would participate than you might imagine. But let me urge the use of ThoughtForms for this purpose. You remember, Mom, the last night I spent with you on your plane?"

I knew immediately what Karen meant, though I had never been sure until that moment whether she had been aware of the action I took that night. She had never mentioned it through Reverend Daisley.

At one time during her last day, Karen's Dr. Irwin had explained that all hope was gone for her. Yet he had also warned us that there could still remain many days of vegetable existence for her. She had already been in a partial coma for some time. That night, she talked to me and asked for permission to leave; I knew I should not hold her back. If possible I should help, but not physically. Never that for me.

Without consulting Tom, I made the most important decision of my life. I spent the rest of that night praying for Karen's quick and painless release from her suffering. I was not sure what awaited her, but I was convinced nothing could be worse for her than being a vegetable. I asked those who had gone on before, if they still existed, to welcome her. The next day Karen slipped quietly away from us with no apparent struggle.

Even at the time of this writing I was still uncertain whether my efforts had actually aided Karen's transition. I was plagued by the thought that I might have done the wrong thing, though later Tom insisted it was an inspired action. When my emotions calmed after reading Karen's last statement in the writing, I let the pen continue.

"Your method of releasing me did work, Mom, and is by far the most humane one to use. That night, in your need, you created a ThoughtForm that reached this side with impact. You contacted high souls, you contacted universal law, and your ThoughtForm was answered.

"There was no blame. Yours was by far the best method of release for a person in my condition. It eliminates pain and confusion, for this is the truly natural way to 'die.'

"Though your means of release is the best method, actual physical release need not be avoided. Use whatever method is least violent, so the individual experiences as little shock and confusion as possible."

When Tom later read this message about euthanasia, he asked about the suicide of one who performs such a killing. "Suppose I had literally taken your life," he said. "Our present laws would demand my imprisonment or death. My own guilt might also have overwhelmed me. In such a case is suicide wrong?"

"It is not wrong," came the answer. "The answer would depend on the person involved. First, if the true motive of the mercy killing is love, then probably the person performing it has a high degree of quality. Such an individual soon recognizes that he has performed a worthwhile service and makes excellent progress here. Certainly no physical punishment is needed on your plane for such an act.

"But let me discuss suicide more generally. Most people believe the act is wrong. Suicides are usually committed by emotionally ill people, people who can't adjust to life's obstructions. Yet such adjustment is crucial to gaining quantity. Any shortcut to acquiring quantity in such a case is a serious failure. When such a suicide arrives here, he recognizes his failure. Such recognition can retard his growth in our world for long periods of time.

"Those who take their lives for the purpose of escaping severe physical pain or extreme physically caused depression usually make an easier adjustment. It depends on the spiritual development there. For a person of high quality who has acquired much quantity, the adjustment is smooth. Such an individual rarely commits suicide until his suffering has reached an intolerable level. If one is of lesser quality, the adjustment will be more difficult, and such a person usually takes the step long before it is necessary. This premature release can cause a more difficult transition.

"The aged often take their own lives. Society is frequently to blame for not providing worthwhile work or companionship for them. When one is no longer useful (and I mean literally, not just from a subjective view), or has no human interchange, she can no longer develop quantity. Self-release into the unobstructed allows the person to continue to evolve.

"The key to the problem of suicide and euthanasia, rests on the quantity and quality of consciousness. If these are developed, if obstructions limit growth, the individual is ready for the transition."

"Why has this not been said before?" I wanted to know. "And aren't you afraid some people will take advantage of your view?"

"It *has* been said, but not often in the Western world," was Karen's answer. "Most mediums color the ideas with their own opinions. Until you experienced my passing, your own opinions would probably have blocked such a message.

"Those who would kill others maliciously will not be concerned with this message. Those who would kill themselves neurotically would do so no matter what anyone said. We have *not given these people permission* but have warned them of possible serious consequences. Those who are truly ready for release may be freed by this message, and if this happens, we have performed a service."

I asked about abortion. I would have thought Karen, a modern woman, would have been entirely pro choice. Her answer not only surprised me but has made me rethink my view.

She wrote firmly. "The individual bit of consciousness is born at conception, not at earth borning. Hence, any destruction of a fetus is not only an aborted individual life but an aborted opportunity for evolution. Of course the unborn fetus comes here and develops on this side, but it is always sad when the opportunity for the development of quantity is deprived.

"In some situations, the taking of a new life might be necessary. The mother and the child cannot both survive, and a decision is made in favor of the mother. If others are dependent on her for her aid in their own development, this might be a wise choice.

"Each situation must be decided on its own merit. In recent times pro choice activists make the statement that the state has no right to make such decisions, and they are right. But the woman who says, 'It's my body to do with as I please,' is ignoring her responsibility to another conscious entity and to the whole of evolution.

"Decisions about abortion should be based on the criteria regarding quality and quantity of consciousness. When one of two lives must be sacrificed, ask who will suffer least by being deprived of earth experience. When no sacrifice is necessary and the abortion is only solving a problem of convenience, by all means the entity should be allowed to develop quantity on earth.

"That which furthers individual and total evolution, best solves any problem concerning the transition called death."

18
CHAPTER

TWENTY-FOUR YEARS AGO Karen became the first of The Three Musketeers to cross into her new world. Twenty years later, after a long illness, Tom joined her. This chapter sums up some of the happenings between those crossings.

In the spring of 1975, Karen's childhood dream, and mine, came true: we became authors together.

From the first day of Karen's passing, I had thought about telling the story of the young woman who died two days before her wedding day, of her courageous fight against Ewing's sarcoma. Yet who would want to read so sad a tale? On December 26, 1970, after our first sitting with Reverend Daisley, the happy ending became clear: Karen was still with us. I determined to tell that story.

Tom and I continued to visit with Karen through Daisley, three more times the first year. Our daughter had left home, and we were greedy for her "letters and phone calls." Furthermore, each visit gave me additional evidence with which to convince potential readers.

After two years of automatic writing, the manuscript was ready for a publisher. Finding one proved difficult at first. Nonetheless, many times in the writing, Karen had told me she would see to getting the book published. "Spirit world wants this book before the public. We will see that it happens."

A Hollywood agent took the manuscript, and I began my long wait for results. It took me four queries to find out that in nine months he had sent the manuscript to only one publisher. Where was the spirit world when I needed them? However, I had to trust.

I decided to try out the book on a friend, Barbara, who firmly believed in life after life. Barbara liked my book. "It will bring comfort to many people," she said. "You could send it to my niece, Mary. She's an editor at Doubleday."

Again I waited.

Meanwhile, Tom had heard of another psychic who lived within thirty miles of our home. Although I was content with Karen's messages through George and my own pen, Tom by this time worried that George knew us too well and his messages might no longer be accurate. He wanted confirmation about Karen's continued happiness from another medium. We found one named Sylvia and made an appointment.

Sylvia put aside her household chores and sent the kids out to play. She sat with us in the living room of her tract home. She entered a trance and was controlled by Elizabeth, an Irish nun of the eighteenth century. This nun did all the talking. I suspected that Karen would have preferred to give her messages directly. However, once again our girl came through, giving her name and the message about the single red roses, her car, her dogs. Then Sylvia/Elizabeth said, "Who has written a book?"

I raised my hand.

"It will be published and in bookstores within a year. You will get confirmation soon. When you get the contract, you (she gestured toward Tom) will have concerns, but go ahead and sign. There is no problem."

Soon after, Mary wrote to say she had found a publisher. The contract arrived. Tom did have concerns over one part of the contract, but we worked it out with the editor. I happily signed and thus fulfilled the psychic's prophecy.

❀ ❀ ❀

As the publication date came closer, I had some qualms about the very personal story Karen and I had told. How would people react—in particular my colleagues at Chaffey, intellectuals all? They could be condescending, even snide, if they disapproved. However, I heard nothing but praise from these people. Doubtless any skeptics were polite in my presence. One English professor, who typically disputed any theory he disagreed with, said to me, "I enjoyed your book. I absolutely believe what you wrote. I have a dear friend who took his own life not long ago, and he also has been in touch through a psychic."

The public responded positively as well. Within weeks letters began to arrive. Most people simply said, "Thank you. You and Karen convince me there is an afterlife."

Heartbreaking letters came from some who had lost children. "Since Karen says she helps children across, would you ask her if she knows Johnny?" I asked, of course, but I wasn't a test medium like Reverend Daisley. I couldn't produce the kind of specific evidence that could convince a grieving parent. I tried to answer such letters with that explanation and with the assurance that if Karen had been greeted and cared for, their child would be too.

I usually urged them to locate a psychic or see Daisley. Many lived too far away to come to California, so I found the phone number of the American Society for Psychical Research. Often people there could recommend a medium in a given area of the country. Gradually I acquired the names of specific mediums that people at that time told me were good. A few people made special trips to California from Iowa or Minnesota just to sit with Reverend Daisley. He and their loved ones never let them down.

Some letters from people who had lost children discussed the causes of their deaths. Karen died in 1970 at the height of the hippie movement. Many parents of young people described the deaths of their own children from drug overdose, sometimes deliberate suicide. These families needed reassurance. Karen's response satisfied me that even the suicides were accidental deaths and the person was usually not directly to blame.

She consulted with people in her world and said, "My colleagues here tell me that of course we are all responsible for our actions. They would urge young people not to use drugs. But the actual deaths in most of these cases were accidental. Parents should not blame the child or themselves. Recognize that humans err, that they and others can learn from these errors, that in my world the balance can be restored and the person can become whole and useful again."

That made me ponder her own passing. When we finally got Karen into the hands of Dr. Irwin, her oncologist, he told us that there was a slight possibility she might have acquired the Ewing's sarcoma from blood transfusions when she had plastic surgery on her nose. By that time we knew that Ewing's was a form of cancer with a high percentage of fatality. I asked her, "If you had known you could get cancer that way, would you have had the plastic surgery?

"Probably. I was so vain, I doubt that anyone could have talked me out of it."

Later, in the automatic writing, she said, "I know now that I would have taken the risk even if I had known I might die. I am only too human. It might help you to know that just as we inherit genetic predispositions, we also have at birth spiritual predispositions through the quality and quantity of the purpose we serve. These spiritual factors have far more influence in determining when a person will come to this plane than any single decision we make on earth."

❧ ❧ ❧

Tom had worried that we might be contacted by weirdos. I knew he could be right. To help control the possibility of harassment, he had our phone number unlisted. Occasionally someone called the college. Secretaries there never give out employees' home phone numbers, so I could return calls or not at my discretion.

About six months after the book was published, a young man I will call Robert Rodgers, phoned from a city in Northern California. His message said he wanted to ask me some questions about the book. I returned his call. I soon learned that he really wanted to visit Karen's home. "Now that we are married, she said I can live in her room."

Oops!

I returned no more of his calls, so he wrote that he had married Karen, that she loved him dearly, that she had told him that we would be delighted to have him live with us. His proof? A joint bank account in his name and hers, which still appeared to be Karen Walker, not Karen Rodgers.

I didn't answer his letter.

Another letter announced that he would arrive at the college at 11:00 A.M. on June 3. He would show me proof of their marriage at that time.

Tom had a class until 11:30, but he rallied the troops. He asked several men in the Language Arts Division to be available to help protect me—just in case. Students must have been dumbfounded that morning to see five male English teachers standing about in the patio rather than sitting in their offices.

Although Robert had never sent a picture or described himself, I knew who he was the minute I saw him. About six feet tall, blond hair, nice looking, briefcase in hand, he walked up the hill from the administration building. I motioned for my faculty protectors to wait. I asked, "You're Robert Rodgers?"

He smiled. "You knew me. Karen said you would." He reached out as though to embrace me. Five men took a step toward me. I stepped out of his reach.

"I didn't know you. You just don't look like a student."

He shrugged, put his brief case on a bench and started to open it. Five men took another step closer—waiting for a gun to appear? He pulled out a marriage certificate with his name and Karen's and handed it to me. "I told you we were married."

"That is not Karen's signature. Not even close. Besides Karen still loves Jim."

"Not any more. She said she never really loved him."

He ignored my "Nonsense" and produced a check book with her name printed on a check. "We have a joint checking account."

I shook my head. "Anyone can have checks printed."

"But she's spending the money. See, here are the canceled checks with her signature on them."

The top check was made out to a gas company. "That is not Karen's handwriting nor her signature," I said. I took the initiative. "Exactly what do you want from me?"

"Karen said you would be my mother."

"Karen would never say that."

The chairman of Language Arts came to my rescue. "I'll have to ask you to leave now and stop bothering Mrs. Walker. She has told you clearly that she doesn't believe you."

Robert looked around. "Not until I talk to Tom. He's my dad. He'll listen."

At that moment Tom came out of class. "No he won't," he said.

Tom took Robert's arm. "Where are you parked?"

"I came on the bus."

"Then I'll walk you to the bus stop."

As they went off down the hill and the teachers moved toward me, I sank down on a bench. They asked, "Are you all right?"

I had to admit I had been nervous—and angry. I thanked them and laughed in relief at their witticisms about writing a book that attracted weirdos.

Later Tom told me that he had told Robert to get lost. "He won't be back, I'm sure. In fact, he was more pathetic than aggressive." Tom even found the situation amusing, as had our colleagues.

Of the hundreds of people who wrote, this was the only strange one; the rest were caring and loving.

Some readers wanted more information about Karen's new world. Does Karen live in a house, eat in restaurants, have possessions?

About houses and restaurants, Karen teased, "You think I live in a barn, maybe?" Then she said, "With your limited view of the universe, you have trouble imagining our world. As I told you in earlier writing, time and space as you know them are limitations for you. We have fewer obstructions because we have bodies that are of finer substance, higher frequencies, less cumbersome than yours. Yet we are recognizable as individuals, and we clothe ourselves in raiment of light and color. I told you once that I am lighter, and you wondered if that meant literally light comes out of us or if we are made of lighter substance. The answer is *both*.

"You ask if I have possessions and if I eat candy bars. I can if I want. For a while after some people arrive, they still want the things they enjoyed there. I have a few of my most wonderful treasures. Bobo, for example. He's the first stuffed animal I ever owned. He no longer has any fur, but I still love him. And I made a duplicate ring of the ones you and Dad made from my Chinese coins. Sure, I still have possessions.

"But before I had been here very long, I found out that the candy bars of your world can't begin to live up to the 'desserts' here. The best way I can explain is to say that we have the essence—the most important ingredient—of everything you have."

She continued, "I don't want to get so detailed as to describe houses and such. Do you remember reading *Raymond*, by Sir Oliver Lodge?"

Karen had directed us to this book. In that writing, the famous British physicist had described contact with his dead son who discussed living in brick houses and smoking cigars.

She said, "That's too specific. The idea is this. Think of the essence of houses and eating in restaurants. You live in a house for protection, privacy, and comfort. We have the same needs, and we have ways of achieving these—but not necessarily in a brick house. You eat in restaurants for convenience, and usually for companionship. So do we in our way." Again she teased, "Of course I eat out; I'm my mother's daughter.

"Yes, I still love to read, but it's not the same here. We absorb thought differently, more directly, in ThoughtForms. Reading is not so time-consuming for me as for you, but I do enjoy the totality of the experience. Just as you love the touch and smell of a book, just as you love the acquisition of information or the pleasure of a good plot, so do we." She refused to elaborate further.

Often when I would ask a specific question, Karen would "go find out." Occasionally the answer would have required that she travel far. Finally I asked. "You seem to travel considerable distance very quickly. Is that actual?"

"Of course. I can be *there* in an *instant*. Think about what is involved in getting from here to there in your world: time, space, and motion. Your body must somehow move through *space* in rapid *time*. You compress this process when you choose to drive a car instead of walking, or when you take a plane instead of driving. You manipulate the obstructions of your world. Because our bodies and our world are unobstructed, we can manipulate even more effectively."

The question I thought of sounded dumb, but I asked it anyway. "Do you have some sort of ethereal airplane?" I giggled at the picture of Karen flying about on a carpet or floating on a cloud.

"Nothing so clumsy," she gloated. "See if you can figure this out. In your world, sidereal time (time determined by means of the stars) controls your time measurements. You also have psychological time. How do you manipulate time without using any devices of any kind?"

I tried out an answer. "With my attention, I suppose. When I'm totally bored with a lecture, one hour seems like three. When I'm interested in weaving fabric for a new dress, an hour seems like five minutes."

"Exactly. We too have our versions of sidereal and psychological time. In addition we have ThoughtForms. Because Thought-Forms are literal for us, we use them to actually manipulate the essence of time."

"Hold on," I protested. "Explain *essence* of time."

"You had no trouble with the essence of a house—to provide protection, privacy, and comfort. Get rid of the idea of time as a continuum. The basic quality of time is to contain events. We perceive it as a receptacle. Time receives, without measurement as you know it."

I got that, I thought. "If time isn't linear, there is no need for measurement, only for being."

Karen agreed.

I tried to conceive of space the same way. "The essence of space isn't linear either?" I asked. "Space moves things? Is that its essence?"

"Not quite. You're ignoring motion. Motion moves things. Space conducts."

"So space is the conductor of things. And motion is the impetus that makes the receiving and the conducting happen?"

"Very good. Time receives. Space conducts. The impetus of the motion is something we've talked about before—frequency."

I worked on that. "Let's see if I can figure out how you use these. We manipulate time, space, and motion; you manipulate receptivity, conductivity, and frequency. Is the "manipulation" anything like what we do when we make time and space seem shorter or longer?"

"Yes. But our manipulation is more real."

"ThoughtForms!"

"Exactly."

I asked a few more questions, but could get no more information or clarification.

"Sorry," Karen said. "If I get too specific, the ideas will get obstructed. Besides, it's more fun if you experience it for yourself someday."

I had to be content with that.

Many correspondents saw Karen as a potential friend. Sometimes young people saw her as a role model. One young corespondent wrote, "I'm an only child too. My parents say I'm spoiled. Was Karen?" Who am I to say? Tom and I certainly tried to avoid spoiling her and urged her to be independent.

Several asked if she had ever taken drugs. I'm sure she did

not. She never even took a glass of wine or beer and didn't approve when Tom and I did. If Karen had a flaw it was pride in her intellect. She valued her brain too much ever to do it damage. One semester at Chaffey College, a professor had an end-of-semester party for his students. Someone spiked the punch. Unaware that it contained vodka, Karen drank several glasses, became ill and vomited. She was not only embarrassed but angry as well—that anyone would take liberties with her body and mind that she would not take herself. Did this kind of thinking make her pious? I think not. She had her own sense of self and values.

Some asked, "Was she religious?" Yes and no. She disliked Sunday School. We didn't make her go. I had been a minister's daughter myself and did not want her to feel the same pressures I had experienced, to be a perfect person. When Tom became too sick to remain in the ministry and she could attend a school where no one knew her past, she was clearly relieved. She always told her new friends that her dad was a teacher. She went so far as to tear the labels off the magazines that came to the house addressed to Reverend Thomas Walker so no one would know. But she was religious in a personal way. Something deep inside her was spiritual.

❀ ❀ ❀

Though *Always, Karen* has been out of print for many years, occasional letters still arrive. These often ask about the currently popular recounting of near death experiences (NDE). I am asked, "Why didn't Karen talk about going through the tunnel and seeing the light?"

I passed that question on to her. She said, "My purpose wasn't to describe such an experience. That may seem important to those who return to your world. I focused on feeling good and being free of pain after a year of nothing but pain. Also, I wasn't being given the option to stay here or return to your plane. I was to stay, and I knew that. My job was to adjust as rapidly and easily as possible. Being a perfectionist, again my mother's daughter, I set about the task of learning to adapt to my new condition."

She went on, "I did tell you some of the accompanying experiences described by those who returned to your world. They talk of getting the same sense of loving presence here that I felt at my arrival.

"Second, although some people experience seeing the tunnel and light, the crossing is not identical for everyone. Even the recountings of people who return to earth plane describe differences. Perhaps the most important aspect of the NDE is to recognize its parallel with the birth experience. Babies are born by being ejected through the mother's birth canal (tunnel) into light and loving warmth (earth environment and parental arms). Both are birth experiences. I now have two birthdays: January 12 when I was born there and December 17 when I came here. Please celebrate both with me.

"Third, those NDEs often include the idea of a premonition of disaster or death. Mine was drawn out over a period of a year, but it is a common part of the experience of dying. What we learn is that dying is not a disaster at all.

"Fourth, many describe communicating with beings who give advice and help the person decide whether to stay or return. Some describe this individual as Jesus; others use other descriptions. Do some talk to Jesus and others to someone else? The best information I receive here is that each earthly participant interprets this person or persons in his or her own way. The Christian is likely to see the figure as Jesus, although one would have to wonder why one good Christian soul is escorted about on this side by Jesus and another equally good Christian soul gets a substitute. Does a Buddhist see his guide as Buddha? The point is, these persons are real, wise, loving, forgiving, kind, accepting."

❀ ❀ ❀

Many people wondered why Karen doesn't seem to talk about Jesus or God. I asked her, "What is religion like on your side?"

She said, "The same as it is on yours—a variety of beliefs and contradictions." I felt the pen chuckle at that point. Nonetheless, she gave a serious answer. "When we come across, we are the same people here that we were there. We don't change our beliefs. The person who was raised in a particular faith, usually remains in that faith—Catholic, or Baptist, or Jehovah's Witness. The Jew remains a Jew, the Buddhist, a Buddhist. Those beliefs and rituals remain satisfying.

"However, as people experience the larger universe, they often find themselves expanding their ideas to a more encompassing kind of spirituality—a concept of the interrelationship of all being. Such expansion leads them away from specific sects and denominations. Some continue to perceive a relationship with a being they call God; others see this being as a universal force for oneness in the universe. But make no mistake, whatever we believe, we are even more spiritual here than we were there."

Although I maintain my friendship with Reverend Daisley, I haven't tried to contact Tom through him or anyone else. I know he is with Karen and cared for.

Tom is around. He does his part. A week after he died, I couldn't bear to see his big white car in the driveway. On my morning walk, I said, "Tom, I'm going to sell your car, but I have no idea how to go about it. Help me." The next day I felt compelled to wash it and hang a *For Sale* sign on it. I sold it the following day at a good price, for cash.

Both he and Karen occasionally step into my life to help, though Karen does the talking. Most often she chats with me as I take my morning five-mile run.

One morning Karen interrupted my run. "Check on your annuities," she said.

I postponed any action. The next week came an announcement in the mail that one of the insurance companies holding a large sum of our family annuities was in trouble. I wasted no more time, consulted my CPA, and rescued the money.

The same thing happened just this year when Karen warned

me about a potential problem with my bank. I moved my funds to another bank just before I learned that the bank Tom and I had used for thirty years had folded.

Karen and Tom also took charge of getting *"More Alive Than Ever . . ." Always, Karen* published. Karen had guided the events that led to its original publication in 1975; in 1994, she apparently determined to get this sequel published. During those twenty years, Karen had continued to take over my pen. When I started using a lap-top computer for writing, she continued to take control. I get the same tingling feeling in my hands and arms when she does. She actually controls my fingers on the keyboard. The computer does work more swiftly than the pen.

"Mom," she said one day, "sometimes I've read over your shoulder, and you've written some good stuff over the years. I like your historical novel. You should try to get that published."

Karen's control of the keyboard stopped for a full minute, then she continued. "You should get the sequel to our book published first. I have a plan, but it is too complicated to try to explain here. Just stay open to suggestions."

I waited, and I continued writing the novel as well as a book about Tom. Meanwhile I taught advanced composition classes at Chaffey College and supervised the part-time English faculty of thirty-five people. When I prodded her about publishing, Karen would only say, "Be patient."

Then came the phone call from the research producer of the television show "Unsolved Mysteries." "This is Hilary Roberts. I just read your book, *Always, Karen*, and am interested in using it for a segment on the show."

"Ridiculous. That was twenty years ago. My life is different now."

When she said, "Karen's message is even more timely and relevant today than it was when she gave it," I decided to let them film an episode. That effort eventually led to the writing and publication of this book.

Karen performed some amazing manipulation of people and events to make that happen. When she makes a promise, she keeps it.

On those days when I miss my loved ones the most, I know that some day The Three Musketeers will see one another again.

Twenty-four years have passed since I last saw and touched my daughter. She has now lived longer in her new world than she did here. Can I picture her as she might be if she had remained here? By looking at my own skin turned to crepe, I can imagine small wrinkles about her eyes and mouth, her auburn hair less vibrant. Although those images haze over, I know that the inner Karen would be the same: innate sweetness refined, mischievous wit sharpened, knowledge expanded, intelligence enhanced, discernment developed. I loved her then; I would love and admire her now.

She remains *always* Karen.

Bibliography

Doyle, Arthur Conan. *The New Revelation*. New York: George H. Doran Company, 1918.

Jung, Carl G. et al. *Man and His Symbols*. Garden City, New York: Doubleday and Company, Inc., 1964.

White, Stewart Edward. *The Unobstructed Universe*. New York: E. P. Dutton and Company, 1940.

About the Author

JEANNE WALKER has taught at Chaffey College in Southern California for more than twenty years and was chairperson of the Language Arts Division for four. As Professor Emeritus, she teaches advanced composition and literature classes, supervises and mentors the part-time English faculty of thirty-five instructors, and writes articles for professional journals.

Photo by HAHN THI PHAM

152